PRAISE FOR

LETTERS TO A YOUNG FARMER

"The chance to make a difference in quality of life for all depends on the soil and those who care for and nurture the earth. New young farmers are on the front lines in the struggle for survival, the future of our children and theirs."
 —**Neil Young**, Farm Aid

"This will make you want to become a farmer."
 —**Mark Bittman**, author of *How to Cook Everything*

"An extraordinary harvest of wisdom from a ragtag crew of farmers, cooks, and agitators—and a must read, not just for young farmers, but for anyone with an interest in a robust food supply in our era of climate chaos."
 —**Tom Philpott**, food and agriculture correspondent, *Mother Jones*

"What a wonderful gift this book is to all aspiring farmers—full of sage wisdom, passionate encouragement, and practical advice from some of the greatest food and farming heroes of our time. Their words will inspire and remind you why farming is indeed the most important work to be done."
 —**Naomi Starkman**, founder and editor-in-chief, *Civil Eats*

"Young people face a steep and uncertain climb on their journey to farm. *Letters to a Young Farmer* is fuel for the moments when they might turn back. With love, respect, and a hearty embrace, the book's authors show a new generation of farmers that their work is at the very foundation of life on Earth."
 —**Lindsey Lusher Shute**, executive director and cofounder, National Young Farmers Coalition

D0030529

LETTERS
TO A
YOUNG
FARMER

ON FOOD, FARMING, AND OUR FUTURE

STONE BARNS CENTER
FOR FOOD & AGRICULTURE

Martha Hodgkins, editor   Illustrations by Chris Wormell

PRINCETON ARCHITECTURAL PRESS · NEW YORK

"We started out to save the family farmer. Now it looks like the family farmer is going to save us."
—**Willie Nelson**, Farm Aid

"You are so young, so much before all beginning…have patience with everything unresolved in your heart and…try to love the questions themselves as if they were locked rooms or books written in a very foreign language. Don't search for the answers, which could not be given to you now, because you would not be able to live them. And the point is, to live everything. Live the questions now. Perhaps then, someday far in the future, you will gradually, without even noticing it, live your way into the answer."
—**Rainer Maria Rilke**, from *Letters to a Young Poet*, 1929

PUBLISHED BY
Princeton Architectural Press
A McEvoy Group company
202 Warren Street,
Hudson, New York 12534
Visit our website at www.papress.com

© 2017 Princeton Architectural Press
All rights reserved
Printed and bound in the United States by Thomson-Shore
20 19 18   6 5 4 3

ACQUISITIONS EDITOR: Rob Shaeffer
PRODUCTION EDITOR: Sara Stemen
DESIGNER: Paul Wagner

SPECIAL THANKS TO: Janet Behning, Nicola Brower, Abby Bussel, Erin Cain,
Tom Cho, Barbara Darko, Benjamin English, Jenny Florence, Jan Cigliano
Hartman, Lia Hunt, Mia Johnson, Valerie Kamen, Simone Kaplan-Senchak,
Stephanie Leke, Diane Levinson, Jennifer Lippert, Kristy Maier,
Sara McKay, Jaime Nelson Noven, Joseph Weston, and Janet Wong of
Princeton Architectural Press —Kevin C. Lippert, publisher

LIBRARY OF CONGRESS CATALOGING-IN-PUBLICATION DATA
Names: Stone Barns Center for Food and Agriculture | Hodgkins, Martha,
editor. | Wormell, Christopher
Title: Letters to a young farmer : on food, farming, and our future /
edited by Martha Hodgkins, Illustrations by Chris Wormell.
Other titles: On food, farming, and our future
Description: New York : Princeton Architectural Press, [2017]
Identifiers: LCCN 2016013820 | ISBN 9781616895303 (alk. paper)
Subjects: LCSH: Agricultural literature—United States.
Classification: LCC S494.5.A39 L48 2017 | DDC 630.973—dc23
LC record available at https://lccn.loc.gov/2016013820

CONTENTS

STONE BARNS
CENTER FOR FOOD
& AGRICULTURE

This anthology was organized by Stone Barns Center for
Food and Agriculture, a nonprofit organization
on a mission to create a healthy and sustainable food
system that benefits us all.

A portion of the proceeds from the sale of this book
supports Stone Barns Center's Growing Farmers Initiative and
the Berry Farming and Ecological Agrarianism Program.

stonebarnscenter.org
berrycenter.org

INTRODUCTION

I want to go home.

Not to the house that I live in with my husband and children, but to the place where I grew up and where my roots are firmly planted. I don't know what drives my instinct to return to this place. But maybe my deep attachment to northern Michigan, where my parents still live, and my desire to go back there someday are driven by the place as much as the people.

My childhood was spent amid a glacial landscape of gently sculpted hills, deep sandy soils, crisp lakes, and gravelly rivers. Just as geography and climate shaped my world, so too did the industry of generations of family farmers — those who planted orchards of tart and sweet cherries, who cultivated rolling pastures of hay, hunted morels in their woodlots, and managed extensive plantations of second-growth pine.

My attachment to this place lives in memories of kayaking down the Intermediate River, leaf-peeping at Deadman's Hill every fall, and listening to my parents' brass quintet practicing in the kitchen while I tried to do my homework. But among the most powerful memories is one of a farm that lies just outside of the small town where I grew up — a farm high atop a glacial moraine between Torch Lake and Lake Bellaire. It's the farm on the hill where my dad got his Scout stuck for three days in the blizzard of '78. It sits across the road and up the hill from the homes of high school friends.

The landscape of Kalchik farm is carefully tended, as it has been my entire life. But I took it for granted. I did not fully appreciate the kind of care it receives until I had the opportunity to work with imaginative and hardworking farmers like Jack Algiere, our lead farmer at Stone Barns Center for Food and Agriculture. But I did have a sense that Kalchik farm represented a brand of stewardship and a protective spirit that made our community special, for it was managed in ways that were respectful of both the natural environment and the people who live there.

Today, knowing the thought and care that Jack gives not only to the intimate management of our farm but also to the larger landscape of woodlands and creeks of which the farm is a part—knowing this now, when I pass Kalchik farm on visits home, I think about what Mr. Kalchik sees that I do not see when he looks out across that extraordinary landscape. I am not a farmer, as Mr. Kalchik and Jack are, but Jack is teaching me to observe, to look closely and try to understand what the landscape tells us: Weak stems and the arrival of new pests may mean that the soil has too much nitrogen. Weedy pastures rich in docks may be pointing to subsurface compaction of soil and a calcium deficiency. The disappearance of kestrels may warn of too many herbicides applied in fields well beyond our farm. Jack has taught me to listen, to watch, to see, as the poet William Wordsworth said, "into the life of things."

This book, in part, is about learning to see what others, many of them farmers, see—things we don't see or that we take for granted. It's about capturing their reflections and stories, to be shared down through generations. The stories from our agricultural landscapes and heritage hold compelling ideas about feeding people, fostering community, sustaining livelihoods, restoring soil, sequestering carbon, protecting natural systems, and reconnecting us to the land. The letters and essays in this anthology reveal important ideas about food, agriculture, and culture—how patterns of eating and farming have emerged and evolved, and sometimes devolved, and how they need to coalesce now in a way that creates a more sustainable future.

Letters to a Young Farmer, written by some of the most influential farmers, writers, leaders, and entrepreneurs of our time, offers advice, observations, gratitude, and a measure of harsh reality. Farming is a difficult endeavor and an arduous undertaking at best, yet farming remains one of the most important, tangible, and meaningful things one can do to improve human and environmental health and community well-being. And it is vital to our future.

Stone Barns Center was founded in 2004 to create a healthy and sustainable food system. We work on both how food is grown and how it is eaten, and we invest in the people, such as farmers, who are envisioning and building a resilient and sustainable future. On our eighty-acre farm north of New York City, in concert with our partner, Blue Hill at Stone Barns, we bring together farmers, chefs, scientists, entrepreneurs, journalists, thought leaders, and others who can help shape and give voice to a way of eating and cooking that is based on healthy farms, soils, and ecosystems. We work with people—many of whom are included in this book—who care deeply about solving the problems that confound our American agriculture, diet, and food system.

This anthology grew out of our concern for the next generation of American farmers, who are inheriting all the problems created over the past decades and yet on whom we are relying to feed us well into the future. We invited a range of talented and experienced farmers and nonfarmers alike to contribute a letter or essay to this collection. We asked them quite simply, "What would you say to young farmers who are setting out to farm now?" This book is the multifaceted, deeply inspiring response to that question.

Through this collection of voices, we hope to shed light on some of the key issues confronting farming today and on the search for answers. All of the book's contributors are thoughtful and generous with their words—words that articulate their dreams and despair, beliefs and commitment, histories and experience.

In these letters, I hope you will find that the promise of a more sustainable and resilient future has never been brighter, and that the prospects for good food, grown well, are strong. There are big challenges and significant obstacles ahead, but take heart as you soak in these words and embrace their wisdom. Believe in the vision they hold of a future where we value and respect farmers who grow and raise food in ways that treat land, animals, and people well; a future in which we hold farmers everywhere with the appreciation, respect, and encouragement they deserve.

Jill Isenbarger
Executive Director
Stone Barns Center for Food and Agriculture

BARBARA KINGSOLVER

Let me speak to you as a familiar, because of all the years I've cherished members of your tribe. Of course, I also know you're only yourself, just as I remember the uniqueness of every intern, WWOOFer, and summer weed-puller who has spent a season or two on our family's farm. Some preferred to work without shoes. Some were captivated by the science of soils, botany, and pest management. Some listened to their iPods, or meditated, or even sang as they hoed and weeded, while others found no music among the bean beetles. A few confessed to finding this work too hard, but many have gone on to manage other farms or buy places of their own. In these exceptional souls I invest my hopes.

I don't need to tell you what there is to love in this life; you've chosen it. Maybe you've even had to defend that choice already against family or academic advisers who don't see the future in farming. Clearly you do, and are moved by the daily rewards. You like early rising. You can't wait to get outside, cup of coffee in hand, to walk among seeded rows and take stock of the new lives that have risen to meet the day. You'd stay late in the barn with a ewe giving birth, just for the thrill of watching the newborns emerge and make their wobbly first march to the teat, a new family creating itself before your eyes. You'll slog through a deep February snow to enter the summery hoop house, inhale a humid blast of kale-scented oxygen, and smile like a fox, knowing you've mastered time travel here, at least on a modest vegetable scale.

I expect you know you'll have to navigate many kinds of relationships. It's tempting to think of farming as a hermitage, and it's true you'll sink deeply into one place, learning by heart the insides and edges of its weather and soils. Its pollinators and birdsongs will be the poetry and music of your days. You'll have a stormy, long-term relationship with a troop of deer or a dynasty of groundhogs. You'll need a good dog. But your life will be full of people, too— sometimes so many as to drive you a little crazy—as you foster your own tribe of interns who come to you with unformed agrarian ideals. Give them enough work to sort out the able from the unsuited, and whet their ambitions. Look around for mentors. Traditionally, farms passed down through generations, but at this point in history, that's not likely to be your case. It will be up to you to find your farming family, people who can teach you how to make smart choices and forgive your own mistakes. You'll meet long-timers at conferences, and if you're lucky, in your own neighborhood. Even if some of these old-schoolers have approaches that strike you as outmoded, they stayed on the land when everyone else was leaving it, and for this they deserve respect.

Of course, the majority of people in your life won't be producers but consumers: the happy you-pick families and CSA subscribers, the hard-to-please chefs and retailers, the farmers' market patrons. Their ignorance will alternately entertain and aggravate you. They won't understand what to do with your kohlrabi, or why you can't hand over turkeys in November that they didn't order in April. They'll want to know why your tomatoes cost more than the ones they buy at the store—the ones picked by exploited labor, grown on some faraway land that's being poisoned to death. Try to explain. Once will not be enough. Be patient, because you need these hungry people as a musician needs listeners, as a writer needs readers. To them you owe the privilege of doing the work you love.

It probably goes without saying that you'll need to study, keep good records, keep your eyes open, and respect the complexities of your profession. It's a bold business in which you will partner with your ecosystem in everyday acts of creation. People have been doing this for as long as we've called ourselves civilized, and that doesn't mean it's easy. That means your profession has a history, a philosophy, a body of science, and whole libraries of accumulated wisdom. As the world changes, you'll have to learn not just the old ways but new ones, how to cope with new kinds of droughts and floods, the critical importance of sequestering carbon under your crops and grass-finished livestock. You can read the modern innovators—Eliot Coleman, Joel Salatin, Wes Jackson, among many—who are rescuing your profession from decades of mistakes that masqueraded as modernity. And the scientist-philosophers whose wisdom exhorted us all along to avoid those mistakes: Sir Albert Howard, Rudolf Steiner, Lady Eve Balfour, Masanobu Fukuoka, Rachel Carson, Aldo Leopold, Wendell Berry. You'll have to work these into your curriculum between the more urgent readings of veterinary manuals and tractor repair guides. I hope you didn't choose this job because you disliked school. You're still a student, and your homework will never end.

This is getting at the heart of what I want to tell you: however calloused your hands, however grimy the uniform, however your back may sometimes ache, you are a professional. Your vocation is creative, necessary, and intellectually demanding. Unfortunately, you'll run into a lot of people who won't see you that way. You're the offspring of a generation—mine—that largely turned its back on the land and its benefaction. We, in our turn, were raised by a generation that set itself hard to the project of escaping from agriculture. For the latter half of the twentieth century, the official story was that modern ingenuity could mechanize farming so efficiently, a handful of folks could oversee the process while everyone else fled the tyrannies of farm life and rural stultification. Legions believed that story, trained their sights on the city lights, and never looked back. Or they were heartbroken at the prospect of forsaking their family livelihood, but still were forced by poverty to leave the farm for the factory. In any case, they counseled us, their children, to stay in school and study hard so we could score a respectable life sitting at a desk indoors and never get dirt under our fingernails at all.

The subtext of this message is that manual labor is degrading and that soil is, well, dirty. Some people will see your coveralls and presume, at best, a countrified backwardness, and, at worst, a deficit of smarts or ambition. It's a hateful bigotry, as wrong as equating those deficits with dark skin, or femaleness, or a Southern accent. (And I'll add here, if you are a female Southern farmer of color, I dearly hope you've found an online support group.) Prejudice runs around unchecked in surprising quarters. I know kind, well-educated people who happily patronize their farmers' market but recoil at the idea of their offspring becoming farmers. It will take time for your profession to recover from decades of bad press. Whether you like this agenda or not, your career is going to be a sort of public relations event, in which you will surprise your market customers not only with your flawless eggplants but also with your intelligence, industry, and good grammar. This might be just the mother in me talking, but if you show up clean, it will help.

In exchange for your efforts, we will learn to respect the art and science of your work. We'll be grateful for your courage and your vision. Prepare to rectify one of the most ridiculous, sustained oversights in all of human existence. When we told our youth that farming was a lowly aim compared with becoming teachers, doctors, or lawyers, what were we thinking? We need teachers for just a few of life's decades. If we're lucky, we'll see a doctor only a few times a year, and a lawyer even less. But we need farmers every single day of our lives, beginning to end, no exceptions. We forgot about that for a while, and the price was immense. Slowly, we're coming back to our senses. Be patient with us. We need you.

Barbara Kingsolver's thirteen books of fiction, poetry, and creative nonfiction include the novels *The Bean Trees, The Poisonwood Bible,* and *The Lacuna,* winner of the Orange Prize for Fiction. Translated into more than twenty languages, her work has won a devoted worldwide readership and many awards, including the National Humanities Medal. Many of her books have been incorporated into the core English literature curriculum of colleges throughout the country.

AMIGO BOB CANTISANO

I am one of thousands who moved to the country in the "back-to-the-land" era of the late sixties and early seventies. I am one of the few of that once-popular movement who survived, thrived, and is still farming. In my forty-six years of organic farming, farm advising, and activism, I've learned a few things that may be useful for you. I wish to share them in the hopes you will be able to stand on the shoulders of your elders and in the sincere wish that you will be one who is thriving forty years hence.

But first, congratulations and thank you for joining us! We agrarian elders are thrilled to see the rising interest in agriculture from young people. After decades of an ever-increasing aging in the organic farming movement, it is a great relief to see the vigor and excitement of youth being demonstrated by all the new farmers attracted to the agrarian effort. It gives us farmers and activists great heart to know that our efforts were fruitful in stimulating the next generation to return to the land. We are so grateful you are with us.

While there is genuine excitement and positive change taking place in agriculture, it is tempered by challenges that are real and potentially debilitating to this burgeoning movement. In this essay, I hope to identify some of these, as well as your opportunity and responsibility to address them successfully so that your important efforts are truly sustainable.

Economics. While the demand and interest in local and organic food is at an all-time high, it is all too apparent that the economic constraints associated with small-acreage organic farming are as daunting as ever. It will require great adaptability and perseverance on your part to be economically viable. The pressures from so many directions are still stacked against the family farmer. It is essential to establish enduring relationships with your customers and create a personal relationship with your audience, not only for the satisfaction of knowing who is enjoying your food but also so that you may present compelling arguments about your need to earn a real living from the food you provide. This may require many forms of communication and outreach, in a nearly nonstop effort.

Do not consider yourself a failure for having a difficult time making a real profit in agriculture; it's rare. You or your significant other may need off-farm income to sustain your farming addiction. In a recent survey in our rural county, 92 percent of the farms had one or more principals earning money off farm. When we first started farming in the mid-1970s, we lived so far below the poverty line, I didn't know it existed, but we made a commitment to profitability, which even to this day is elusive. You and I are not in this for the money—that's pretty obvious—but we need to strive to truly sustain this life. If you provide the best quality and live up to your commitments, you deserve strong consumer support, and that includes receiving a price that rewards your efforts. I am in awe of those who continue to push prices up with their audience, educating them about why it is so important to support local, family farms. Make your voice heard!

Skills. As you well know, farming requires a wide array of skills. Rarely have any of us entered into farming with all the skills necessary to be successful. The actual growing, as complicated as it is, is only part of what you need. I urge you to acquire all of the necessary skills, including labor management, bookkeeping, equipment repair, long-range planning, carpentry, record keeping, integrated pest management, weed identification, fertility analysis, computer skills, and all the rest. There are so many balls we need to juggle today, and we usually don't have the resources to hire others who specialize in those skills. We need to become accomplished generalists. If you don't have those experiences and knowledge, you may need to attend courses, read books, study online, and learn from others in your community. As everything is constantly evolving, continuing education and training will be necessary. Use the opportunity to learn from fellow farmers, both young and old.

Using the experience of elders. My friends and I are amazed at how rarely the young farmers in our community connect with us to learn what we have experienced and how we may be of assistance. Many of us have been farming for three or four decades, and we have learned much from trial and error, eventually creating success. It is unnecessary for you to repeat our trial-and-error process; it's complicated and expensive, and we offer our experience, much of it learned from mistakes, to speed the process of your successful farming. Please don't be hesitant to ask the elders in your community for advice, including those who farm conventionally. Many conventional farmers are extremely skilled at the basic practices necessary for all farms. We all have something to learn and share. We might be able to offer you some valuable advice, help you troubleshoot, or work with you to develop your farming system. Some of us are willing to lend equipment or teach you how to modify yours to maximize its potential. There's a lot to learn from us geezers; don't be shy. We're usually happy to help.

Cooperation. Going it alone is too difficult, while working with others has so many benefits. I have noticed that too many farmers see their neighbor farmers as competitors, a phenomenon that continues to this day with younger farmers. Many of us agrarian elders have learned the benefits of cooperation and collective involvement. My advice is to look to your neighboring farmers as allies working toward the common good, rather than as competitors. Sharing equipment can be challenging but may be the most economical way for younger farmers to accumulate the appropriate tools. Sharing experiences and knowledge is essential. Sharing a meal creates community, support, and bonding.

Activism. We have noticed a general lack of youthful participation in the bigger-picture issues surrounding agriculture. It is *essential* to participate in your agriculture and general community in order to keep the foundational efforts of the agrarian elders alive and moving forward. I urge you to be involved with local farm groups, organic certifiers, ag activists, political activities, celebrations, events—anything that you think can effect the evolution of agriculture. Yes, it can feel overwhelming just to maintain the farm; however, if all of us had felt that way and did not participate in the bigger picture, we would be much poorer for it. Many of the things you see as normal today required many hours of volunteer efforts to migrate from the fringe to the mainstream of American consciousness: farmers' markets, cooperatives, organic standards, direct marketing, efficient equipment, new crops, seed saving, genetic preservation, financial and legal support by government, the buy-local movement, support for small farmers, conferences—all are the result of diligent efforts of many farmers volunteering their time to move our society forward. There is so much more that needs to be done—with plenty of opportunities for you to participate. It's absolutely essential. Please step up and take the reins from the older generation to shape and improve the future.

Experimentation. Farmers who are endless experimenters operate the most successful farms I know. They don't assume that what was successful last year or five years ago is the solution of the future. With the evolution of varieties in most crops, it is essential to try new releases and compare them to both varieties that you are familiar with and those that are the mainstays of the species. Doing your own breeding and seed saving can be very rewarding. Crop rotation, cover crops, composting, biological control, equipment utilization, irrigation, propagation, pruning, and many other processes are all in need of evolution. In taking the opportunity to challenge your assumptions, you will grow. Sometimes growth will come from failure, so experiments should be kept small to not jeopardize your finances.

Community. Our society is still poorly informed and connected to its food and its farmers. Outreach is essential for the continued health of the farming community. I challenge you to reach out to your neighbors and larger community in an ongoing effort to educate and engage. Some of the most successful community experiences I've participated in include farm tours, on-farm educational programs, radio and press interviews, harvest celebrations, social media and online outreach, food bank and homeless support, horticultural therapy, and more. All of these add complexities and time to an already busy schedule, but it's critical for all of us to continue to educate and stimulate our clientele and neighbors.

Tenacity. I'm pretty sure that all of us have periods when we doubt the viability and desirability of our work and lifestyle. The life path we have chosen is a hard one, both physically and mentally, and often financially too. I've had long periods of contemplation, wondering why I have chosen such a challenging life, but I have always come to realize its importance to me and to my community. I can't say I haven't thought about throwing in the towel a few times, especially after particularly difficult years involving bad weather or other calamities. But then I remember why I do what I do: it's next to impossible, and I thrive on the challenge. I'll bet you do, too. When things get tough, I encourage a conversation with an elder farmer, who will likely be willing to share how he or she made it through the tough times. Please remember that the few of us who are still farming are the survivors of a much bigger slice of our population, most of whom left farming in the last seventy-five years. Sharing with and learning from those survivors can yield great rewards—and more than a few laughs!

Observation. In my experience, the best farmers are the best observers. The more you look and ask, the more you will see and understand. Stop and smell the roses and observe them at the same time. What are they trying to tell you? What can you learn from them? How can we coax more cooperation and productivity out of the plant and animal world? What actions are we taking that are stimulating and nurturing to the environment? What might be hurting more than helping? What else can I do? How do plants respond to my care? There are miracles unfolding right before your eyes and under your feet. If you have a great memory, you'll remember them. If you are like most of us, keeping some notes will prove invaluable. I have had the privilege to observe crops and the environment on hundreds of farms as an organic farming adviser over the last thirty-five years, and I learn something virtually every day—even more as my observation skills have improved. I thought I knew it all in my twenties; man, was I wrong. I have more curiosity and questions now than ever. So may it be for you.

Adaptability. It's important to be able to adapt to changing situations. I started out as a row-crop farmer, but as I've gotten older, I have changed my farming focus more toward perennial crops. For the first twenty-five-plus years, I leased farmland, so my ability to have a long-range plan for perennial crops was nonexistent. In 2000 I purchased a small piece of land, and I've subsequently changed my focus to perennial crops, both because they are so needed and important in our community and also because they fit the ecological profile of this land better than row crops do. Perennial crops are easier on my body, as well.

Marketing. I've also adapted my marketing methods to the evolving ways that we can reach consumers. Most of our production in the seventies and eighties was intended for wholesale. Consumers had very little interest in local, organic, or family-farmed products, so it was not effective to market directly to them. Since then, we have made increasing efforts in direct marketing, both to consumers and to those businesses that have a sincere interest in our local family farm production.

What does the future hold? I'm not sure, but the trend toward appreciation of organic and local food is a healthy one and will continue to expand. Creating direct relationships with consumers and chefs just makes good sense, but it will require adaptation. In much of California the competition has gotten so strong that numerous new farms are excluded from farmers' markets unless they offer unique products or are willing to sell at less profitable markets. Restaurants are now used to six-days-a-week produce deliveries, many offering organic options, so we have to work harder to keep their business. CSAs, long-championed as saviors of many small farms, now face increasing competition from specialized delivery businesses that emulate the consumer connection of a small CSA, but with the economic advantage of a bigger and better-financed operation. And regular chain stores now feature "local" products and "farmers' markets," further clouding the picture for the average consumer.

You will need to adapt to the changing patterns and fickle purchasing habits of your marketplace. What's hot today may be icy cold tomorrow. Keep experimenting, looking for new crops. Ethnic crops have a huge market potential. Visits to foreign countries will open your eyes to many foods that can be profitably grown. Palates and trends evolve. From the fifties to the seventies, I knew only one other family who ate pesto, a staple in our house. Now it's everywhere. Salad mix was nearly unheard of in the eighties in the United States, yet was already popular in Europe; look at it today. I couldn't give heirloom tomatoes away in the seventies and eighties; now people pay a premium for them. Edamame, sushi, and Asian greens are fairly recent migrations to mainstream US culture; there are many other examples. Tastes change. Farmers who adapt early have the opportunity to profit and thrive.

Us versus them. There has been an unfortunate yet long-lasting dynamic between organic and conventional growers, and between smaller and larger growers. This clash has been debilitating to the success of all agriculturalists. It is essential to recognize that all scales of farming, and all methods, still require many decades of evolution to achieve true sustainability. It's important to remember that those who are farming with chemicals or on a large scale are doing so because they believe it is essential and necessary. Few farmers today feel comfortable using chemicals, but they are often unaware of viable options. Their precarious economic conditions prevent them from transitioning away from chemical dependency; they operate from a fear-based mentality that sees farming without the aid of pesticides and other chemicals as too risky and dangerous. I believe that more than 90 percent of the successful transition from conventional to organic is confounded by the farmer's psychological makeup rather than the technical obstacles. Most of agriculture, and most of our society, has been brainwashed to believe that the solutions and opportunities for ecological success are out of our control. The magic "remedies" that have been sold to our culture over the last seventy-five years, in combination with a full-court press of misinformation provided by academia, corporations, and ag media, have created an illusion of powerlessness that is very deep-rooted and extremely difficult for many farmers to wake up from. Farmers—big and small, conventional and organic—are all allies, no matter where we are on the continuum of "purity." Please do not fall into the trap of judging those who use chemicals or farm on a large scale as being wrong. The issue is too nuanced to be addressed through a "small-is-good-and-large-is-bad" or "organic-is-good-and-chemical-is-bad" ideology. We in agriculture are an endangered species, and it does not benefit anyone to belittle or condemn those who have not yet seen the light. Please reach out without judgment to those who are not entrenched in the beliefs that you hold so dearly. You can be their mentor and ally and learn from them as well. It's time to see *all* farmers as one extended family. We are all in this together and need to support each other for the collective evolution of humans.

Act locally, think globally. All of your actions, no matter how small, can have a huge impact on the environment and on the humans that it feeds. Every step we take to improve the ecological stability and sustainability of our farms will have long-lasting impacts. The ability to sequester carbon is still poorly understood; however, we know that by increasing the soil's organic matter, we can have a positive impact on climate change. We know that using few or no pesticides positively impacts ecosystems and human health. We all need to continue to work diligently to improve the quality of the soil, air, wildlife, and the earth. This is a continuum, with much progress still to be made and urgently needed. You're not alone in your understanding and concern for the issues of the day. Please share what you know and grasp for new meaning. As you work on your farm, please consider your obligation and opportunity to affect all beings, everywhere. The future of the planet depends on it.

Taking time for family and self. Too many farmers, myself included, have not succeeded in the important area of maintaining mental and physical health for themselves and their families. Many of us work too many hours and take too little time for our loved ones and ourselves—with major implications for the emotional and physical well-being of our families and ourselves. While you're young, I urge you to set aside regular time for yourself and your loved ones, as no work regime is more important than your emotional and physical health. My observation is that the younger generation is doing better at raising children than my generation did, but the demands of agriculture can limit our ability to fully care for our loved ones. They grow up so fast, and if you want them to do so in a way that is most healthy, take time and share the roses with them. You'll be so glad you did.

In closing, I wish to reiterate my gratefulness to you for joining us on this long and vital journey. Persevere and you will thrive. When all else fails, please remember that laughter *is* the best medicine! Keep on keepin' on. I gotta go, the farm is calling...

Amigo Bob Cantisano has farmed a wide range of small- to medium-acreage organic crops in California since 1975. He founded California's first organic farm supply, first organic farm–advising service, and first organic farming conference, among numerous other agricultural accomplishments. He currently farms eleven acres of diversified food crops in the Sierra Nevada of Northern California and advises on more than forty-five thousand acres of organic and transitional crops throughout the Western Hemisphere.

WES JACKSON

As a young farmer within an industrial society, you are farming in a social context similar to that of the Green Revolution—the intense push by foundations, governments, scientists, and others in the latter half of the twentieth century to harness science and technology to substantially increase agricultural production around the world. Once you join with your heart and mind to act on the necessity of an ecological agriculture, you become a target, similar to the farmers of the less-developed countries who were targeted in that revolution, which transformed much of the planet.

Over the past half century, countless grain acreages in Asia, Africa, and Latin America experienced yield gains as much as two- and sometimes three-fold. Genetics and plant breeding, fertilizers, pesticides, and irrigation made it possible, of course, but seldom mentioned are the implicit and explicit assumptions behind that bushels-and-acres effort. Those roots go back to the early 1940s, when increased production helped calm the politics of Mexico; arguments about distribution versus productivity had played a role in the election of Mexico's president, Manuel Ávila Camacho, in 1940. Know that. Know also that few people seem to know that the press invented the term "Green Revolution" to stand in contrast to the "Red Revolutions" of the time. Know also that the Green Revolution needed promoting, that the market alone could not make it happen. Therefore, a campaign was launched to gain institutional support, requiring great coordination backed by Rockefeller money. Almost from the beginning of the Green Revolution and all along the way, as environmental historian Angus Wright has explained, the following underlying assumptions emerged:

1. Low productivity—yield per acre—is the problem. Soil degradation was factored in, but only as a cost in the emphasis on the input/output ratio. The gap between the social and the scientific was more or less ignored by the big players.

2. Traditional farming techniques are more of an obstacle than a resource. So the new equation took shape: "We (the experts) are the teachers; they (traditional farmers) are the learners."

3. Technologies are neutral. So when persuasion fails, it is time to use compulsion.

4. Agriculture is to serve as an instrument to achieve industrialization. Adoption of the Green Revolution package became essential. (Need more agricultural chemicals? Build a chemical plant.)

5. Agriculture is not vitally linked to nature.

The Green Revolution required public support. But today, given more private engagement in agriculture, the belief is that the market will find solutions. Emphasis on intensification now reigns. To be fair, greater consideration is being given to the ratio of inputs and outputs, and we are now willing to say that social considerations must be given much higher priority, thanks to a small closing of the gap between social and scientific cultures. Back then (less so now), techniques of traditional farmers were regarded as more of an obstacle than a resource.

Why is all of this relevant to you as a young farmer? Even with all our recent gains, the momentum of that past is still with us. In fact, field size has expanded—which means that if your farm is small, for all practical purposes you will be largely ignored by those, including our government, who accommodate the big players.

If you try a few traditional techniques that worked in preindustrial agriculture, the county agent will be of little help to you. He or she will lack even the brochures that are standard for conventional farming support.

If you avoid, for whatever reason, modern technologies—position planting, Roundup Ready seeds, whatever—you may hear, one way or another, that technologies are neutral; they are benign and cause no unintended harm. You will encounter more than a residual assumption that *agriculture is not vitally linked to nature*. If you are an organic farmer, you will be regarded as marginal. If you deviate from the latest technology, you will be regarded, at best, as "interesting."

On the line in our time is an ecological worldview struggling to replace the industrial mind, as we embrace nature's wisdom rather than rely on human cleverness. As a young farmer, you have great potential to be an agent of change. What that means to you in an operational sense, of course, will depend on your circumstances. But know this: farming in an ecological way is a major part of a mandate for global ecological change. It won't be easy, but if we don't achieve sustainability in agriculture first, that overall change will not happen. Squiggly light bulbs and Priuses, whatever value they have, come out of the industrial mind. Ecological agriculture has the disciplines of ecology and evolutionary biology to call on, based on millions of years of emerging efficiencies such as those seen in nature's prairie ecosystems. The industrial sector has no such organizing discipline to call on.

Wes Jackson is president of The Land Institute, which he co-founded in the 1970s after he returned to his native Kansas from California, where, as a professor, he had established the Department of Environmental Studies at California State University, Sacramento. He is the author of many books, including *New Roots for Agriculture; Nature as Measure; Consulting the Genius of the Place: An Ecological Approach to a New Agriculture; Becoming Native to This Place; Altars of Unhewn Stone;* and *Meeting the Expectations of the Land*, edited with Wendell Berry and Bruce Colman.

CHELLIE PINGREE

If you are a young farmer today, thank you. If you are thinking of becoming a young farmer, thank you. Without you, we can't make the changes that so many of us believe are critical to reforming our food system, and we certainly can't reverse the devastating damage that has already been done due to our changing climate. We need you; we really, really need you.

By "reforming our food system," I am talking about making it possible for more and more people to include healthy food in their diet, making it possible to have more of our food grown without toxic chemicals, and making farming practices that preserve our soil become the standard and not the exception. It means sending fewer herbicides and pesticides into our water supply and less pollution into the air. And it means supporting a food distribution network supplied with more food grown by the farmer down the road—and less food from a truck driven halfway across the country.

From where I sit, I know that consumers want things to change, and I can see that their demand is changing the market for what you are growing faster than any public policy I can promote. I know that as young farmers, you are in the right place at the absolute right time. The products you can grow will change our system, and the very act of farming and providing food to consumers will be the basis of how we push new policies.

Nothing is easy about the act of farming. I have been a farmer much of my adult life, so I know this; but I also know that the rewards are great.

Maybe you are starting out farming in the same way I did. I was the most unlikely young person to become a farmer. I was only a teenager when I moved to a small island off the coast of Maine in 1971 and became a "back-to-the-lander," trying to grow my own food. Even though my Norwegian grandfather had immigrated to the United States for the opportunity to farm in the dark, black soil of southern Minnesota, I had grown up in the city of Minneapolis. By the time I left there, I was more interested in protesting the war and rejecting authority than becoming a farmer. And I certainly didn't picture myself living in a small, rural community like my ancestors did. How wrong I was about it all.

But this isn't an essay about me. Really, it's a letter to you about what I have learned over the first sixty years of my life and what I am still learning that might be useful for you to consider when thinking about being a farmer. There is so much I could write about: how to decide what animals or plants to grow or what farming methods to use or markets to develop. I could write about what it takes to make your farm profitable or how to make sure you care for the land in a sustainable way or how to make sure the work you need to do can possibly fit into the hours in a day. But I want to look at only one part of what you do: the importance of the political act of being a young farmer.

I assume you have chosen to farm because there is something you love in the act of farming. This includes the ability to work at a craft that requires you to understand and know so much—from weather patterns to soil science, the physiology of the plants you grow, and the habits and nutritional needs of the animals that will graze in your fields. It requires an appreciation of the repetitive tasks—many that need to be done day after day, year after year—like feeding the chickens, weeding the carrots, watering the lettuce, harvesting the tomatoes, milking, shoveling, washing. It means checking the cold barn in the middle of the night or waiting up for the lambs or piglets or kids to be born, just in case something goes wrong and you need to be there to turn the baby so the mother can finally end her labor and start nursing the next generation.

I don't want to attach some false romance to the work of a farmer, but there is some beauty to the repetition, and mostly you need to love it all enough that you can approach it with a calm appreciation. In that way, while your hands work, your brain is free to observe and calculate to determine what needs to be done next and what will make your farm a better operation. That is what will make you feel successful at what you do and what will make the work of farming feel rewarding and pleasurable. But if the chores really all feel like chores to you, perhaps now is the time to turn back.

In Maine, where I live, people are returning to farming, which is reversing the trend of people moving away from farms—a trend that had been going on for many, many years. This return is part of the idea of farming as a political act. And consumers are increasingly searching out food that they believe will be more nutritious for them and their families. As there have been more opportunities for them to find this food, they are choosing the healthier, better-tasting options so they know what they are getting.

This is all good—because it means that if you choose to be their farmer, you will have grateful consumers who will appreciate the many hours you spend providing them tasty, healthy food grown in an environmentally sound manner. It means you have a better chance of being paid well for your hard work and your skills that have made it possible for those wonderful tomatoes or melons to come from your farm.

It wasn't this way when I started out as an organic farmer. Saying that I was an organic farmer was more likely to draw ridicule than an interested crowd wanting to know more. It wasn't easy to find an agriculture school with a sustainable ag program or a store that would buy our produce and place an organic label on it. Luckily, I had a market to sell to; I lived in a grateful rural community where I had an endless supply of customers. Not all of them had high incomes, but they were so grateful to have fresh eggs or a glass bottle of milk with cream that would rise to the top or sweet corn that hadn't traveled for days before it was cooked in their pot or tomatoes and peas bursting with flavor. I knew I was appreciated from the first day I harvested a leaf of lettuce.

I started as a farmer but quickly became interested in the politics and policies of food. Over the past forty years, I have seen a tremendous amount of change. In the early 1990s, more than twenty years after I first began farming, I was elected to the Maine Legislature. I served on the Agriculture Committee, and, while there were bills before us to label GMOs and bills to ban, or just label, the presence of bovine growth hormone in milk, they were not supported by many legislators of either party. The debaters mostly ridiculed the supporters of organic standards—anyone who thought we should have restrictions on pesticide drift or labeling requirements of any kind. Consumers were not entitled to that much information; they would just get the wrong idea!

Today I approach these issues as a member of Congress, where I keep my focus on changing our food system and changing our farming practices. While members like me who believe we should label GMOs are still ridiculed at times, and we can't quite win the vote on that issue, when it comes up, our office receives thousands of calls and emails from informed consumers insisting that they have the right to know what is in their food. It gives me such hope to know that the consumer is demanding, the marketplace is changing, and people who serve in jobs like mine in Washington, DC, or in state legislatures across the country are hearing a little more every day about why they need to be on the side of change if they want to represent the people who elected them.

But none of this change will happen without young farmers. In the end, the most political act of all starts with you. In a way, it is so simple—just proving every day that you can grow the food that we all want to eat and want to feed our families. I can stand up to make the most eloquent and articulate argument about why we need to do things very, very differently—but unless you are there, with your delicious tomatoes at the farmer's market, filling up the CSA boxes every week to supply the families of your community with healthy food, and selling the chickens you have proven can be grown without antibiotics— unless you are there, someone can always say, "That's nice, but it can never happen." Thanks to the growing number of young farmers who are daily lending their hard work and creativity to finding a better way to grow our food, I believe we can make it all change.

Chellie Pingree lives on the island of North Haven in Maine, where she is a longtime organic farmer. She has represented Maine's First District in Congress since 2009 and is an outspoken advocate for federal policies that better support sustainable farming.

VERLYN KLINKENBORG

Most of the farmers I've ever known—and all of the farmers I've ever known well—were family members: grandparents, uncles, aunts, cousins. In my memory, they're so different from each other that it's hard to say what unites them, apart from being kin and working on the land. They seemed monumental to me when I was a child, people of a stature that a townsperson in Iowa could never possess. What gave them that stature I can't wholly say at this distance, now half a century later and so many of them gone. It was strength, hardiness, a capacity for endless labor and invention, but also a certain saltiness of mind and—I'm thinking of aunts and uncles now—a habit of speaking ironically. My dad once or twice tried to explain why he, the fourth son of a prosperous farmer, didn't become a farmer himself. I suspect it was because he didn't understand irony—how to hear it when it was being used around him, how to employ it in conversation.

I've seen photos of all of them young. I know they were young once, and some of my cousins I knew when we were youngsters together. But it's hard to imagine any of those farmers being truly young in the ways it's possible to be young today—or that I was young then. They grew up with too much responsibility. They had their own version of the quiet, profound air I often see in ranch kids, who understand the consequences of things: a gate left open, a water line frozen, a thrown shoe. I don't mean to suggest that my farming kin were unduly sober. Every farm kid I knew growing up seemed to have a wild side, except when it came to the serious business of farming. Put the two together—a certain wildness of heart and an unerring sense of responsibility—and you end up with men and women who understand irony.

When I first wrote about farming—in a book called *Making Hay*—I was surprised to discover that I had somehow earned the respect of the farmers in my family. I was surprised because I thought I qualified, at best, only for their affection. I was a nuisance on the farm. I feared the machines. Many of the animals also scared me. Out in the countryside, I sometimes saw weary, humorless farmers living on bleak farmsteads that were lit at night by yard-lights staring blindly down at rutted farmyards. These were farmers who were going under. I was surrounded by the consequences of things, but I never did see them until it was too late—and only after they were pointed out to me. I looked at the skills my young cousins had—good mechanics all of them—and it seemed like they'd simply been born with them. I wondered sometimes whether they were ever explicitly taught how to do the things they knew how to do—and why I missed all that teaching. But then I remembered. They grew up on the job from the first day there was a job to fit them.

Their letter to young farmers is the one I'd like to be passing along to you— the one my grandpa or my uncle Everon or aunt Janelle might have written. I can't imagine what it would have said. They weren't, as a rule, advice-giving people. They could tell you what to do, if needed, but otherwise they assumed you had common sense, which, if you're lucky, is a wellspring rising artesian within you. They told stories about people who needed advice, and it was clear, if you listened between the lines, that needing advice was a state to avoid. When I came around while writing *Making Hay*, I asked over and over the questions they never expected to have to answer, questions like when and how much and how and why. In time, I think they began to enjoy answering me. It was a summer full of delicate, almost fragrant ironies.

In the absence of that letter—*their* letter—I'd like to point out a few things. Perhaps you'll find them worth thinking about. The farmers I grew up around were rural people. They came from the very spot they later farmed or just a few miles down the road. They didn't come from cities or suburbs, nor did they go to them, much. They didn't choose to farm. Choosing would have meant choosing *not* to farm. Their educations were shaped around the fact that they would be farming one day, which is to say they were educated almost entirely on the farm, though most of the men were also leavened in the military. Farming was never once, in their long lives, fashionable.

They were conventional farmers. To the extent that they innovated, they tended to innovate toward greater mechanization, higher yields, less time in the fields, and skillful use of the increasingly complicated financial tools they were offered. In the century and more that my relatives have been farming in northwest Iowa, they followed the fundamental arc marked out by the

USDA. In that world, as it happens, survival and success turned out to be one and the same.

Are these the conditions that lead to the best kinds of farming? They are not. My aunts and uncles (my father, too) were born into a socially rich and culturally ambitious countryside full of farms and small farm towns. Over the course of the twentieth century, the rural population plummeted. Families vanished, and their farmsteads were plowed under. As social and biological diversity dwindled, so did democracy. (Plot together, if you will, the decline in species and rural votes per rural acre in Iowa between 1915 and now.) This is an ongoing tragedy of largely unexplored dimension. The history of farming in Iowa over the past century looks like the grimmest kind of evolutionary struggle. What makes it worse is the ease with which the illusion of choice has been preserved.

Perhaps you don't need a theory of free will to farm well. Perhaps you don't need to understand the intricacy of what it means to be rural to think of *rural* as a construct defined by forces far beyond the control of the people who actually live rural lives. Perhaps it isn't necessary to try and see all the ways in which you're bound to a system that follows its own imperative without hesitation and with no regard for your welfare. But I think it makes all the difference. To farm well now, at this moment in history, you need to be radicalized, again and again, every day, to turn yourself into that rare figure, the "practical radical," to borrow a phrase from William Cobbett, the nineteenth-century English farmer and reformer.

Recently, something has swept many young people into farming. The moral energy behind it—and, yes, the fashion—makes it possible to believe that this new agricultural movement is more powerful than it really is. Will there come a moment soon when the energy lapses and young people—who have grown up, most of them, in a world of innumerable choices—are swept just as rapidly out of farming? Will they choose again and choose differently? I see it happening already. What matters in this movement—what makes it so precious—isn't merely technique or philosophy. It is the welcome return of farmers to a depopulated and denatured landscape. For once it has been tilled, the richness of the soil depends upon the social and cultural wealth of the community that lives upon it.

That sounds like a metaphor, but it isn't. I mean it quite literally. I suppose it's possible for the kind of social and cultural wealth I'm talking about— a collective wealth, surely—to be embodied in some monumental individual.

That person—he, or as likely she—resembles the "future farmer" who shows up to guide us around his Wisconsin farm near the end of Aldo Leopold's hopeful but still vital essay "The Farmer as a Conservationist," which was written in 1939. Leopold is portraying the good farmer of his best hopes, the one with a care for the past as well as for progress, who has a profound respect for the diverse workings of nature and the wisdom of elders and the teachings of science. Individuals like that come along from time to time. But it's more practical to imagine those virtues embodied not in a single person but in a community of farmers, which is the very thing conventional agriculture has been killing as long as I've been alive.

Verlyn Klinkenborg is the author of several books, among them *Making Hay, Timothy; Or, Notes of an Abject Reptile*, and *Several Short Sentences About Writing*. He teaches at Yale University and lives with his wife, Alexandra Enders, in New York City and Columbia County, New York.

KAREN WASHINGTON

———

Dear young farmer,

I am writing this letter because I am concerned about the future of agriculture. I see in your eyes the eagerness to grow food, but also I see your hesitation. Look, I know that farming is hard work—not a glamorous profession, to say the least. But we have come a long way from the shame and scars that haunted us a mere century ago.

I say to you, young farmer: go with your instincts and your heart. Our ancestors have never left you. Listen closely to the beating of your heart, the rhythmic patterns of breathing, the tingling in your hands as they reach deep, deep into the soil. Never forget that you come from an agrarian people— people who knew how to grow food and take care of the land. It has been a symbiotic relationship, the love of land and Mother Earth.

Listen in the early morning as the birds sing out loud, designating a new day. The dew lies softly on the earth and covers the plants. Smell the fresh air, crisp and cool. Yes, young farmer, you are one with the earth. What stories will you tell your young? How will they know of a people who were denied their forty acres and a mule, but kept on defying the odds to find land to grow food?

I am getting old now; have fought many battles along the corridors of food and social justice, a mere pittance to those who continue to combat the evils of racism; and although you can't see the chains and shackles around your hands and feet, make no mistake: the trauma still exists. But you already knew that. From the first day you took your breath, you knew you were special. You knew that the road to success would be long and arduous. Like a tree bending in the wind whose roots are strong, so too are yours.

Young farmer, learn as much as you can about farming and life. Listen to your elders, for they are wise. They will tell you the secrets of growing food without chemicals or pesticides. They can smell and taste the soil to let you know if it is good for planting or not. Whatever you learn, share that knowledge with others; whatever you grow, share with those who have less. Be prepared to meet the challenges ahead, but know that you are not alone.

So proud I am that you have chosen to be a farmer. Go with my love and blessing. Always remember you stand on the shoulders of greatness, and your love for the land will never be denied.

Love always,
Mother Earth

Karen Washington is an activist and farmer. She is co-owner of Rise & Root Farm in Orange County, New York, and cofounder of Black Urban Growers (BUGS) in the Bronx, New York.

JOAN DYE GUSSOW

I've grown food for almost fifty years—very seriously for at least twenty—but I've never needed to market the products of my soil to pay my way. So I'll start by acknowledging that our stakes in this enterprise are very different. Nevertheless, I hope you'll find what I have to say useful.

In the class I teach about food and the environment, one of the readings is a multipage chart showing the change over time in the number of farms in the United States and the percentage of the total population engaged in farming. Right after Europeans landed in North America, almost everyone did some food growing; they had to if they were going to eat. But between 1790 and 1890, when the new nation's population ballooned from roughly four million to sixty-two million, the percentage of farmers was halved. Yet as the twentieth century opened, well over one-third of the population was still farming. Most people knew farmers; many people had close relatives who farmed.

My father's family had farmed in Iowa, and his oldest brother still did when I was a child. Selling some of the family's farmland helped us through the Great Depression; I can still remember my mother sitting on the front steps crying with relief when the check arrived. But I never lived on a farm.

After the soil fertility-destroying catastrophe of the Dust Bowl and the out-migration of Southern sharecroppers to wartime jobs in the 1940s, the farming population had dropped to 12 percent by 1950. Federal policies, big machines, and the crop chemicals that came to characterize "modern" farming after World War II encouraged the expansion of the remaining farms. "Get big or get out" was the slogan, and farmers did: as farm size more than doubled between 1950 and 1990, the farm population crashed from 25 million to 4.6 million.

By 1993, only 2 percent of Americans were living on farms, and the government concluded that there were too few people actually farming to be worth counting. "Farm residence is no longer a reliable indication of whether or not someone is involved in farming," stated the US Census Bureau in its final issue of *Residents of Farm and Rural Areas* in 1991. "The cost of collecting and publishing statistics on farm residents and farmers in separate reports could no longer be justified."

And today, as farm size continues to increase, though more slowly, and as the number of farms still declines, the average farmer keeps getting older. This farmer was 58.3 in the 2012 census, a continuation of a thirty-year trend of steady aging out. Only 6 percent of farmers are under 35. Which is, I think, you.

To chart the trend of those statistics into the future is to wonder where you might be heading. Economist Stewart Smith, noticing that the declining portion of the food dollar that went to the farmer was tracking toward zero, once asked whether there would be any farming in US agriculture in the years ahead. Indeed, to wander the supermarket today is to begin to ask whether there will be any actual food-growing involved in US agriculture. With millions of acres of our farmland devoted to growing corn destined to feed animals and cars and be turned into sugar, it is not a stupid question.

So where do you fit in? You were born into a world in which very few people had a farmer in their life and "food" was a category that included tens of thousands of items with no recognizable relationship to the soil. I doubt very much that your family raised you to be a farmer. So I suspect you've committed yourself to this profession because you want to grow real food for people, not commodity crops, not raw materials—but food. And although there are still forty thousand items in the average grocery store, you are coming into agriculture when sales of those food-like objects are declining, farmers' markets are multiplying, and another sort of food supply begins to look possible.

Ordinary Americans, even those who have no memories of farmers in their families, are newly interested in these healthy young folks they see at farmers' markets, and they are increasingly aware that farmers, not giant corporations, are the reliable producers of safe and nutritious food. Nationally, we have decided that children need to meet farmers and learn, in school gardens, how food grows. In certain circles, farmers are even considered glamorous, though they themselves know well that the daily lives they lead are not.

All this means that, remarkably enough, you will be privileged to grow food for eaters, not just for corporations, and you will sometimes—perhaps often—have a chance to meet someone who is personally grateful for the crops you produce. Maybe you'll be standing at your stall in a local farmers' market and a grown woman with tears in her eyes will come up and say she hasn't seen a sweet potato like yours since she pulled one out of the ground forty years earlier. So although you're unlikely to make a lot of money doing what you love, you're very likely to make a lot of people happy. Thank you for feeding us.

Joan Dye Gussow, Mary Swartz Rose Professor Emerita and former chair of the Columbia University Teachers College, Nutrition Education Program, lives, writes, and grows organic vegetables on the west bank of the Hudson River. Long retired, she is still coteaching her course on nutritional ecology at Columbia every fall. She is the author, coauthor, or editor of five books, including *The Feeding Web: Issues in Nutritional Ecology, This Organic Life,* and *Growing, Older: A Chronicle of Death, Life, and Vegetables.*

RAJ PATEL

So, dear Sir, I can't give you any advice but this: to go into yourself and see how deep the place is from which your life flows; at its source you will find the answer to the question whether you must create.

—Rainer Maria Rilke, *Letters to a Young Poet*

The Patels are a caste of landowners. My family once were farmers, like you. That was generations ago. Centuries after the British Empire claimed them as subjects, they moved from India, under the rule of His Majesty King George V, to land in the British colonies of Fiji and Kenya. After a generation they, now as subjects of Her Majesty Queen Elizabeth II, fled to London.

There they exploited themselves, as did many others of their name. In London their name means something else now. Patels are convenience-store owners.

I have no advice to offer from the land. I have seen the work of farmers processed into plastic. I have seen my family made wealthy by selling tobacco and high-fructose corn syrup and deep-fried salty things. I have seen my family poisoned by the goods they sold.

I have no advice. But Rilke addresses you as he did the young poet; heed him. Look to the places from which your life flows.

Look to the heavens, and then reckon with this: we will never see Rilke's blue skies. Human pollution has made our skies more yellow, everywhere and for centuries to come. Our eyes have lost a depth of blue. We will see it only in fiction, in the movies; with our eyes closed, in our dreams.

Look to the rains, which fall hard or not at all, coughing life onto your few acres. You will only survive the damage we have done to the sky by farming your soil.

So look to the wellspring of life beneath your feet, to the soil that will save us all.

Look hard at that source of life. When the skies were deeper blue, it was not yours. Before white people came to this land, it belonged to no one, for there was no property in land before conquest. Before white people shackled Africans to this land, cash agriculture had yet to be invented. If you have title to the ground on which you stand, you traffic in stolen goods.

North America is a settler colony, one that has conjured away its history through bullet and ballot. Centuries before you became a farmer, here was an agriculture that slashed and burned and managed the world as if humans were one animal among many. The people of that agriculture, their knowledge, their language, are not dead. They live and fight. Listen for them.

If you want to "see how deep the place is from which your life flows," throw down a pebble and listen hard for its splash. Hear the ancestors of your land; look for the iron of their spilled blood in your soil; turn yourself into a historian of loam.

As a farmer, you're already an agronomist, economist, veterinarian, soil chemist, microbiologist, geneticist, and meteorologist. A new skill can't hurt. But this one should make you uncomfortable.

I am now four generations removed from my ancestors' land. It is worked by others. I have no claim to it. I live in the United States now. But I still remember. I have not forgotten what happened to us, what happened to the planet under European colony and white supremacy. Nor should you.

So look to the place from which your farm flows. Look to your land, and to yourself, and to me, and to those who have wronged us, and to those we wrong, and recognize that for this source of life to endure, we need farming that farms for tomorrow and restitutes for yesterday. Open yourself to that politics, to those voices, to cosmologies in which private property is abusive, and life begins before—and ends long after—you.

Look at the deed to your land, and honor it. The newer ones have ink sprayed on the surface. You can lift the words off with a razor blade. The older ones are intaglio. You can feel the print with your fingertips.

Burn it. Then bury it.

If not that, then at least commit something to a flame—privilege, perhaps. Supremacy. Entitlement. Comfort with the way things are. Whatever it is, look to that which you have burned, and then commit it to the soil.

Follow Rilke's advice. Look to the source of life. Then plant decolonization. Unsettle this colony.

I have no advice. Rilke's is enough for us both. Trace back the life you'll grow to the lives that grew before you. And then imagine a world radically different from this one. One that respects the chain of life that links you to the dead and to the not-yet-living.

That's not really advice. It's an invitation to close your eyes, dream relations of life differently, and work for a blue sky you'll never live to see.

Raj Patel is a senior research associate in the Unit for Humanities at the South African university currently known as Rhodes University and a research professor at the University of Texas at Austin's Lyndon B. Johnson School of Public Affairs. He is the author of *Stuffed and Starved: The Hidden Battle for the World Food System* and *The Value of Nothing*.

BARBARA DAMROSCH

Today I awoke to the first hard frost of fall, with the pastures and growing fields white. The flowers were all dead. Thank God.

I loved the flowers, but the business of tending them, picking them, and turning them into one-of-a-kind bouquets has dominated every week since early April, and I'm ready for a change in my routine. Now I can focus more on writing, while still doing the farm's office work and feeding the crew a big meal on Fridays.

This is the farm's boom time, since we specialize in winter production, but we need our workers in summer too, to grow the crops we'll be selling from root cellars and storage rooms all winter long. So the flowers help pay summer salaries, along with a few specialty crops and eggs from our chickens, until the profitable winter market, supplied with fresh crops from our greenhouses, gears up. That's why we call it Four Season Farm. I would say that ours is not your typical farm, but then I don't think there are any typical farms these days. Each one is different.

Fewer people are born into farming now than they once were, and even if there is arable land in the family, it doesn't always come with parents or grandparents who can guide you. In that sense, we have a generation of orphan farmers. Some go to agriculture school to get the knowledge they need, but many new farmers are drawn to small-scale, organic farming, which is not in the standard curriculum. These farmers learn from reading books, going to conferences, joining one of the organizations devoted to sustainable farming. In our state, it's MOFGA—the Maine Organic Farmers and Gardeners Association. Wherever you live, there is some state or regional group like that. Most offer educational events where you can pick up lots of good advice and trade experience with other farmers, both young and old. MOFGA's Farmer to Farmer Conference is exactly that, since it offers three-hour workshops largely based on information sharing. It's a model worth imitating.

One of the best ways to learn is by working on a farm. If you are just starting out in farming, there are probably only two of you, or maybe there's only you. As your farm grows, you might need to hire helpers, and when you're well into your seventies, as we are now, a few twentysomethings are a great help. We enjoy passing on to them what we've learned in a life of farming. Some of what we impart by example is basic agriculture: how to build a fertile soil and protect it, how to get the best and most productive crops from it and make a profit. But every farmer has his or her favorite tricks; for most of the people who've worked for us, the job is part of a self-styled curriculum in which they try out several farms of different sizes, objectives, and even different climates. It helps them decide what kind of farm they really want to have and where it should be, before they commit to a piece of land. Sometimes being an orphan is a good thing.

Choose a successful farm, and work hard there. The more farm experience you have, the easier it is to get the job, but experience isn't everything. A strong back is good, a passion for the work is good, but the most important qualification is intelligence. A good worker looks ahead, is always conscious of the big picture, and anticipates what the next step will be—but at the same time, follows directions carefully and asks for clarification if unsure of what's expected. The farmers may be too busy to pause and give a lecture, so try to be a sponge, observing and asking questions. Find out how the farmer plans the year, and the year after that.

Acquiring land is often the biggest hurdle for a young farmer. When I got bitten by the farming bug in the 1970s, buying land was out of the question, so I marketed my skills as a landscaper and writer instead. It wasn't until I met and married a bachelor farmer named Eliot Coleman in 1991 that I got my wish. He had bought property in Maine on generous terms from Scott and Helen Nearing in 1968. Scott was eighty-five years old at the time and eager to pass on some of their land to someone young, strong, and enthusiastic to farm it in a sustainable way. This is one good model to follow. Nowadays there are a lot of "farm-link" programs that match would-be farmers with those who'd like to see their land used and improved, either by purchase, lease, or some other arrangement. You might start with organizations such as the American Farmland Trust or Land For Good, but your best resources are likely to be local ones such as land trusts. Just asking around may be the most fruitful course of all. You might also consider alternatives to the single-family farm, such as partnerships; incubator farms; and communal farms in which a group of farmers shares equipment, processing and packing areas, and a farm stand or market.

Whether the location of the farm will give you a good market for your goods is often hard to gauge. Small farms these days tend to spring up around urban areas or vacation spots with an affluent summer population. Shoppers there tend to be food-savvy and willing to spend a bit extra for local, organic, or specialty produce. But there's more competition. Land prices are high. And personally, I'd like to see good food spread around. It might make more sense to go where land and other expenses cost less, even if it means lowering your prices or finding ways to transport your products to markets. I've seen cases where a pioneer in an underserved area can actually attract more food-related enterprises and establish a market for locally grown food where there was none before. Even within our local area, we found that building a mobile farm stand enabled us to find a new spot to sell our goods, and others soon joined us. In the end, it turned out to be our best market.

What kind of farm would you like to have? Unless you have access to a lot of capital, it's obviously better to start small and, as Scott Nearing always urged, "pay as you go." Buying that rototiller, tractor, or electric lettuce spinner will pay off if you take them one at a time and don't saddle yourself with debt. If you want to scale up, scale up. But if a small farm will bring you more personal satisfaction, keep it that way and don't let anyone denigrate it. Many convincing studies done by the United Nations and others have shown that small farms really can feed the world.

Bear in mind, too, that there are no shortcuts when you are building up your soil. If your whole farm is wooded, full of rocks, and infertile, as Eliot's was when he began, it's not going to happen overnight. But a surprising amount can be grown in a small space. One young farm couple who once worked with us started out with a successful microgreens operation on a parent's porch before moving up to more land. Another good crop to grow in limited space is vegetable and flower starts. Shoppers pounce on chemical-free seedlings that are far better quality than the sad, root-bound ones you so often find at garden centers and stores.

Whether you sell wholesale, retail, or both is partly a market decision and partly a personal one. Do you like interacting with customers or would you rather hang out with your sheep? The CSA model, where everyone comes and picks up a box of food on a given day, can be a great compromise and gives you capital up front at the beginning of the season, when you need it most.

It's best to go into farming knowing that it's very unlikely to make you rich. Many young farmers have trouble making a go of it at all. There's nothing wrong with one member of the household taking on an outside job to help pay the bills, either temporarily or permanently. Value-added products add profit to what you grow: jams and pickles, fermented foods, garlic braids, woven goods—the list is endless. The writing that Eliot and I do even falls into that category, since most of what we write is about growing food, and the farm gives us home-grown subject matter!

On-farm businesses work well for some folks because they keep you at home. A farm stand can grow to encompass a small shop or a cafe. An unused barn can host farm dinners, dances, musical events, or lectures. Farm weddings—even quite rustic ones—have become wildly popular. We attended one where a stall full of little, bleating goats provided much merriment and another where a pair of alpacas decided to mate on the front lawn, to the amusement of the guests.

Another way to add income is to become USDA-certified organic. A lot of farmers consider this unnecessary, even when they are practicing organic methods, because people who know them and their farm have trust in them, and the watering down of the organic label has tarnished it in recent years. But while this may work fine at a farmers' market or even a food co-op, a supermarket will give you a better price if it can mark your goods as organic. You might be surprised at the willingness of mainstream stores to sell local and organic goods.

One of the most overlooked ways of increasing farm income is to move into winter production. High tunnels or hoop houses are not as expensive to put up as you might think and they soon pay for themselves. Low tunnels are even cheaper. By focusing on cold-tolerant crops such as carrots and spinach, you might get by with little or no additional heat. For us, using greenhouses as washing, packing, and seed-starting areas has also saved us money. (Eliot's book *The Winter Harvest Handbook* will give you more details.) A lot of growers just want to take a break when winter comes, but how about cutting back on summer work instead or just spreading work more evenly over the course of the year? You'll find a great, untapped market in winter sales.

In the end, though, the best way to ensure survival as a farmer is just to learn to do it better. Performing farm tasks provides ample time for your brain to work while your hands are busy. Always be thinking about how any job can be done more efficiently. Can you modify a tool to work better for you? Could you cut down on purchased inputs by using cover crops for fertility? Do you have enough space to rotate cropland with pasture? Can you grow crops to feed your livestock to cut down on the high cost of organic feed? Can you pay more attention to your soil and thereby increase your yields?

Farmers have always faced these challenges, but I think today's young families have it tough because they are often isolated. In the old farm days, there were grandmothers, aunts, and older siblings to watch a baby, but now the birth of a child takes a parent off the tractor and out of the fields with no replacement, and unless you can find tasks that one of you can perform near the house, the farm may suffer for a while. But people do find solutions. My friend Jen Porter built a sandbox in her greenhouse and swings that hung from the purlins above. Her seven-year-old, Ollie, even grew his own crops of head lettuce that he brought to school and sold to his teachers. My stepdaughter Clara's four-year-old son, Hayden George, collected the eggs, carefully boxed them, and proudly announced the day's total. After a while, farm kids become a genuine help, and there's a sense of family solidarity in farm life. Most parents feel that it's a healthy place for their children, rich in life experiences, whether or not they become farmers themselves.

Come February, the witch hazel will start to bloom outside the office window, and I'll be anticipating the early narcissus that I will combine with it in my bouquets and the black pussy willow that I mix with the first tulips. I'll be swept up in the beauty of it, just as I am every year. Meanwhile, my five-year-old grandson, Pat, has been coming over more, and he loves to pull up carrots, his favorite food. The other day, without my suggesting it, he handed the carrots to me one by one so I could trim the tops. He took some home and demanded a stool so he could wash them himself at the sink. As far as I'm concerned, he's hired.

Barbara Damrosch is a farmer and writer. Her books include *The Garden Primer* and *The Four Season Farm Gardener's Cookbook,* and for twelve years she has had a weekly column in the *Washington Post* called "A Cook's Garden." With her husband, Eliot Coleman, she cohosted the television series *Gardening Naturally* for The Learning Channel. She and Eliot raise vegetables at Four Season Farm in Harborside, Maine.

GARY PAUL NABHAN

———

Dear aspiring and practicing young farmers,

Before anything else, I want to apologize for previously failing to acknowledge your value to our society at large and to more fully support you in gaining traction with your endeavors. In four decades of writing about farming and ranching, I am afraid I have missed the mark by not writing about the issues most critical to your health and well-being. I have been so attracted to helping save the seeds, breeds, soil, and water of food-producing land that I failed to notice that, first and foremost, those resources need bright, passionate, energetic, and innovative farmers and farmworkers if they are to survive and thrive.

So, if you forgive me for my past lack of attentiveness to the most pressing issues you are facing, let me cut to the chase—to the issues of a) making a go of it in an economy that remains structurally adverse to providing a true safety net for young farmers, and b) remembering that farming is more like a spiritual calling than a career or profession.

As one grain grower laconically reminded me, "If you go into farming thinking you'll make money every year, you just might as well drive over to the casino and gamble, because your odds there will be better. Unless you do it because you love it and feel called to do it, whether or not you ever break even, you probably shouldn't become a farmer."

So let me take the second issue first, because I am not very helpful when it comes to economics unless we define what is of value in the broadest sense. As best as I can figure, becoming a farmer is not that much different from becoming a monk, a street preacher, or a contemplative hermit, because it is ultimately about adhering to a spiritual path. You have to have faith that it is your calling because undertaking it does not make much economic, social, or political sense at all. Very few of you will get rich (and stay rich), get famous and powerful, or get laid simply because you are a farmer.

However, you will get paid in being up for drop-dead gorgeous dawns, in seeing trembling creatures give birth, in seeing fruit trees break bud into a bounty of blossoms, and in feeling depleted soil heal into fertility once more. If those are not moments of religious ecstasy that celebrate the incarnation of the Creator in the creation, I don't know what is. Farming can be the Good News made manifest right in your own back forty.

But you'll also need faith in the Creator to survive the hardships: the blasted grasshoppers, the unseasonable freezes, the disease-ridden crop failures, the foreclosures, the arguments with neighbors or business partners, and the heartbreaks among lives living under stress. Notice that I do not assert that you need unswerving faith, because you may need to learn how to swerve even to survive. You may find yourself cursing your god as Job did, but at least choose a god who listens and forgives. You will need him, because most farmers I know (myself included) royally screw up a time or two. Or three or twelve. Or twelve thousand times. Praying won't necessarily be enough to get your tractor or front-end loader out of deep shit. But God helps those who help themselves, whether you use a come-along or a powered winch.

So let's talk economics. Despite tremendous increases in yields per acre over the last half century, farmers today clear no more farm-gate income per acre than their grandfathers did in 1950, largely because the costs of land and inputs have outpaced the higher prices consumers are willing to pay for food. Sure, there are exceptions to that rule, and you'd better aim to be an exception. But a growing number of farmers collapse under the nagging burden of debt, and the suicide rate among farmers—not only in America but around the world—is one of the highest of any profession.

It is above my pay scale to offer you tried-and-true solutions to this dilemma, but I can sure as hell tell you a few things *not* to do. Don't buy expensive equipment if you can borrow or rent it. Don't purchase a big four-hundred-acre farm for its natural beauty if only twenty acres of it are arable and you cannot produce enough to pay the monthly mortgage for the entire four hundred. Have a diversified portfolio of products destined for different markets, but have at least one unique product that restaurants or consumers can't get from other sources. Have some off-farm income.

Furthermore, get health insurance that covers accidents, injuries, and bouts of depression, no matter what. Don't run yourself or your partner into the ground just because it's the American way. Pray, but don't ask the Creator to answer your prayers the very day before the next payment is due. She might get pissed if you try that too often.

The most important lesson that farming imparts to the wayward human psyche is the constant need for humility. It does so by reminding us that we are really not *ever* in control and that we will likely be wrong about the complexities of nature and the economy more often than we will be right.

On the other hand, being a farmer is as close as you can get to being with God, in the sense that you are invited to be a co-creator and steward of a beautiful piece of earth. If lovingly and painstakingly cared for, you will see, that farm will heal its own wounds to produce more bounty and diversity than ever before, and you yourself might be healed too along the way. God forms partnerships with those in other professions as well, but seldom does she invite a mechanic or bus driver or receptionist to be engaged with creation as intimately as she beckons farmers to do so.

I may be extrapolating a little too much from the scant data I can hold in my head and my heart, but I would argue that the Creator has chosen farmers, foresters, and habitat restorationists to be the glue that keeps the world from falling to pieces. We are the connectivity she shaped between the divine and the dirtiness of life itself; between the animal, the vegetable, the mud, and the miracle; between the soil and the soul. This concept is something that the Southern Agrarians like Robert Penn Warren eloquently articulated nearly a century ago, but I sense that it is even truer today.

Bless all your work, and may the Creator place a salve like Udder Balm on all of your wounds, scars, and suffering. May you plow in peas.

Gary Paul Nabhan is an Ecumenical Franciscan brother, a plant explorer, and an orchard keeper of 150 varieties of heirloom fruits and nuts. He has economically failed at about every other kind of farming he has tried. He used to write books before he met Brother Mule in a dark alley. The mule broke him, not the other way around, so now he only writes short poems.

MARY BERRY

When I said yes to being part of an anthology of letters to young farmers, I thought, "Well, finally, a writing assignment that I might be even overqualified to take on." After all, I am an eighth-generation farmer in Kentucky, as is my husband. We are both fifty-seven, which is about the average age of farmers in America. I can't find the average age of farmers in Kentucky, but I know that in our daily comings and goings in our farm community, we seem young! Well, it turns out that being qualified to write something doesn't make it easy to write. In fact, there are so many things that I would like to say to you that I have had a terrible time even figuring out where to begin.

After a couple of months of starting and stopping this letter, I have three dilemmas that I keep running up against, and so I will just tell you what they are. The first is a general reluctance to encourage you to take up what I know to be an incredibly difficult, demanding, and sometimes heartbreaking way to make a living, if you can indeed make a living farming (more about that later). Just choosing to be directly dependent on the weather is challenge enough. But I don't want to discourage a decision to do the best work I have ever imagined, not to mention the most necessary. The second is how different the young people I meet all over the country are from the people I grew up with and started farming with thirty-five years ago. We were generational farmers; we came from families of farmers. Most of the people I imagine reading this letter did not grow up farming. This is not necessarily good or bad—just different. And third, how changed farming is now, at least in Kentucky, from the way it was when I came home to farm all those years ago. And that, finally, suggests a place to start.

After years of being a full-time farmer, I started The Berry Center to continue my family's work in agriculture. Our first public meeting celebrated the thirty-fifth anniversary of the publication of my father's book *The Unsettling of America*. While writing a talk to open the meeting, it occurred to me with much force all that I had to come home to when I came home in 1981. There was a pretty good economy around small, diversified farming in those days, supported by what remained of the federal tobacco program. It was a complicated program whose principal author was my grandfather, John M. Berry Sr., who was himself a farmer and a lawyer. My father, Wendell, has said that my grandfather did the important work and he just took it up. I, in my work at The Berry Center, have now taken it up.

This program for producers was a price support, not a subsidy; it helped to control production with a quota system and took farmers out of a boom-and-bust (mostly bust) economy. Through it, farmers could plan their economic year around their tobacco crop, pay for farms, and have access to operating money. It was the only farm program I know of that did what it was supposed to do: represent the interest of farmers. Because each farm had a tobacco base, or quota, it encouraged farming that fit the rolling landscapes of our farms in Kentucky. For example, our two-hundred-acre farm had a five-acre tobacco base, and we plowed only the least-erodible areas of our place. Around that was perennial agriculture: permanent pasture, hay crops, and a few acres of grain crops for our own use.

The producers' program brought stability to our farming communities. It made possible the handing down of farms from one generation to another, and it kept alive the generational knowledge of how to farm particular places. We bought a farm that was new to us, but we were surrounded by family and neighbors who knew the place and made themselves and that knowledge available to us. (I had to get to be a fairly old farmer to see how generous those people were to us.) I am not sorry that tobacco, with all of its problems, is gone from this landscape, but I am sorry that something like the producers' program doesn't exist to stabilize local production for local markets.

You have entered into an agriculture that is either small and entrepreneurial or large and industrial, with almost nothing in the middle. Some of us are working on putting something in the middle, but it's not there yet, so in the meantime you will have to make your own markets. While you are young and strong, this can be wonderful. By the time you are my age, maybe we will have figured out a way to value people who understand land use and will have some good local food systems in place, so farmers don't have to be completely entrepreneurial.

The odds are that I will not be able to offer to anyone reading this letter the kind of neighborliness and help that was offered to me when I was a young farmer, but I would like to try.

If you were here, I would take you to see what is left of good farming in our part of Kentucky. I would also want to show you examples, and there are plenty of them, of bad farming. But I would caution you to be generous in your attitudes toward what is left of the farming community here. Too much demonizing goes on in the meetings I go to all across the country. There are a good many cultural reasons for what has happened to our countryside and our country people—reasons that you should try to understand as well as you can. You will need to know these things to strengthen your own resolve to farm. The bias against country people and places is real. My father calls it the last acceptable prejudice, and at some point, you will feel it. Those farmers who are farming badly are in an emergency that is not of their own making. You will find out if you farm for very long that it is hard to make good decisions in an emergency.

I would want you to have a chance to visit with my husband, Steve Smith. Steve is a generational farmer who started out farming conventionally and made a change when he saw that he and his farm were wearing out and his debt was not getting smaller. He started the first CSA in Kentucky in 1990. Steve wrote the following thoughts to share with students at the Berry Farming Program a few years ago, and because I can't take you to see him, I will share some of his intelligence:

1. We have substituted fossil fuels for knowledge, and now farmers are cut off from the information we need most: how to build and maintain healthy soil.

2. Most of the information given to farmers these days is sales talk. We must stop looking for store-bought solutions and use what is free and at hand: animal manure, compost, cover crops, crop rotations, genetic diversity, seed saving, natural systems and cycles, husbandry, thrift, frugality, local economics, and local communities.

3. We must rethink the way we market our crops, adding value to them when and where we can. Forming relationships with your buyers is the simplest, easiest way to do this. By allowing your customers to get to know you through CSAs, farmers' markets, direct marketing, and so forth, you add value to your farm products and strengthen the local economy.

4. If you can clear $6,000 or more per acre, how many acres do you really need? Not that many. By using small-scale technology and low-cost and no-cost techniques, you will not need to borrow a lot of money and lots of reasons not to—the most important being that if you go too deep into debt, neither you nor your land will have the last say.

5. It is not simple. The details of the farming operation need to be written down on paper—a working set of plans that includes budgets, crop rotations, seed varieties, planting dates, harvest schedules, buyers, markets, and so forth. The market plan will require the most work. Remember to do your marketing before you do your planting.

6. Farmers need to know that we have very few friends in high places. The global economy does not have our best interest at heart; agribusiness corporations do not have our best interest at heart. We must, therefore, look to those who do: our friends and neighbors, our local communities and local economies.

Are you wondering why I shared this list with you when what Steve has to say is obvious to those of you raised in a local food movement? Steve paid for his farm at a 19 percent interest rate. (Those of us who borrowed money in the eighties remember those interest rates.) He did it by using his head and his imagination and by understanding that he could not pay for his farm and lead the life he wanted to lead without practicing frugality. And this brings me to the hardest piece of advice I need to give. (I said that I would get back to the issue of making a living.)

The problem of upward mobility stays on my mind a good deal of the time. The Berry Farming Program started with Wes Jackson's idea of creating an education for homecoming. Wes says that the dominant major in our colleges and universities for fifty years has been upward mobility, and now it needs to be homecoming. What do young people need to know in order to go somewhere and, as Wes says, dig in? And what, I ask, do they need to know in order to dig in and be able to afford to stay? They will have to see that they will not be able to live what we consider a middle-class life. They will have to get out of the money economy as much as they can by practicing subsistence agriculture. They will have to take seriously the economic value of intangibles. This is what Steve is talking about when he mentions neighborliness and frugality.

A good community is a good economy, made up, necessarily, of people who need each other. This can only happen when its members choose it every day over the siren song of ease.

My great-grandparents lived in a world of limits. My father says that he entered into a world of labor-saving devices and cheap fossil fuel. It took, he says, years of reading, thought, and experience to learn again that in this world, limits are inescapable and indispensable. Steve and I have had to learn the same lessons separately and together. My hope for you is that you see the possibility of joy, contentment, and endless fascination in accepting the limits of your place and whatever community you find and can build.

The talk around the need for a better agriculture producing organic food for more people has been going on for years now. I have been keenly aware of it and involved in the work to make it happen for thirty-five years. In that time, we have lost millions of acres of farmland, and we are down to three-quarters of 1 percent of our American population that is farming. To achieve a saner agriculture, we must have more farmers. To have more farmers, we must ask and answer the question "What will it take for farmers to be able to afford to farm well?"

And so, the work you want to do or are doing is essential. I am grateful to you. Because you might have to look farther afield for a community than I had to when I was a young farmer, consider me your ally. I expect to work to support you and good farming in this country for the rest of my life.

Mary Berry has lived and farmed in north-central Kentucky all of her life. She started The Berry Center in 2011 to continue her family's work in agriculture. Mary and her husband, Steve Smith, raise beef cattle and Large Black hogs in the Little Kentucky River valley.

DAN BARBER

Tell me if you've heard this one before.

There was once a wise old rabbi. One day a troublemaker arrived in town. He challenged the rabbi and made a show of it by inviting everyone to the town square. Facing the rabbi, he held a bird behind his back. "If you are indeed so wise, rabbi," he said, "tell me if the bird I'm holding is dead or alive."

The rabbi quickly realized that if he declared the bird alive, the man would break the bird's neck and present a dead bird; if the rabbi said the bird was dead, he would let the bird fly free.

The rabbi paused before responding. "Whether the bird lives or dies, it's in your hands."

I first heard this story at a religious service many years ago. I've since discovered it's also a Christian fable, and I've read it as a Confucius-like tale (the rabbi is a Chinese philosopher with a flowing, white beard). There is a version with an Italian sage who lives in the mountains and descends into Venice to offer his services, or there's one with a blind wise man and, as told by Toni Morrison in her Nobel Prize lecture, a blind wise *woman,* who is the daughter of slaves.

If you can believe it, there's yet another version, a modern version, reinterpreted and updated, and this one isn't a fable. It goes like this.

Many years ago, Glenn Roberts found himself in a difficult situation. Glenn is not a rabbi, a Chinese philosopher, or an Italian sage. He's a farmer and founder of the artisanal grain and milling company Anson Mills. But back then, he was struggling to sell his first harvest: an heirloom corn for grits.

The seed was remarkable—improved by generations of careful selection— and he was cultivating it in rich, well-amended soils. And Glenn carefully hand-milled the dried corn at cold temperatures to ensure that it was as sweet as the stuff we chainsaw through in mid-August.

But freshly milled grains require refrigeration to preserve their flavor and prevent spoilage, a practice that high-end markets and specialty stores refused to adopt at the time.

"The store managers looked at me like I was from outer space. Refrigerate grits? They had never heard of fresh-milled anything, so the idea that it could spoil, that it *would* spoil very quickly, was absolutely foreign. I wasn't just selling heirloom grits, which people had heard about from their grandparents. I had the flavorful grits *and* the fresh milling process to preserve that flavor. You couldn't have one without the other. No one knew what the hell that meant. Grits were grits."

So Glenn faced a choice: he could kill the flavorful grains by keeping them on the shelf (thereby securing the profit his then-fledgling business desperately needed) or he could pull the corn from the stores and start over.

Glenn told me he came to an answer after considering why he had started Anson Mills in the first place.

The goal of the company—and Glenn's life work—is to recapture the lost flavors of the Carolina Rice Kitchen. The "rice kitchen" wasn't a physical kitchen, and it wasn't about a singular obsession with rice. It was a whole system of interrelated ingredients that evolved out of attempts to repair the depleted soils of the antebellum South. Crops such as buckwheat, peas, corn, barley, rye, sweet potatoes, sesame, collards, and—yes—rice were planted in meticulously timed rotations to improve soil health and produce superior harvests. Lowcountry cooking came together out of this cornucopia, evolving from a supremely advanced farming system. It was, for a while, America's preeminent cuisine.

"The really interesting part," Glenn said, "is that unlike any other time in American history, and I would argue any time since, taste was the determining factor. *Taste.* Even a good-yielding crop—if it didn't taste great, it didn't get replanted."

Glenn's hope was to repatriate not only forgotten seeds and the wisdom of how they were grown but also the technique of fresh milling. Without fresh milling, what was the point of exhaustively researching the most delicious varieties? And why worry about the right order of rotations to better the soil? When Glenn said, "You couldn't have one without the other," he really meant it.

Glenn pulled his grits from the shelf and started over.

❈ ❈ ❈

Today Anson Mills is the premier distributor of artisanal grains in the United States. It coordinates the harvest of thirty-five hundred acres of organic corn, wheat, oats, beans, and many other crops, with annual sales of $4.5 million.

I know, I know, you probably think you *have* heard this story before, or something like it. A farmer stands up to an adversary, whether it's supermarkets or Big Food. Old, regional foodways are resurrected. Seeds are preserved. Organic farming is encouraged. Good food is *saved.* It's a nice fit for farm-to-table dogma. (And this is a movement with a deep inventory of dogma.) The promise is that pursuing the right kind of food reshapes landscapes and drives lasting change.

Except, so far, it hasn't. Well over a decade into the movement, the promise has fallen short. In the last five years, we've lost nearly one hundred thousand farms. Today, 1.1 percent of farms in the United States grow nearly 45 percent of the food we consume. In 2012, corn and soybeans accounted for more than 50 percent of all our harvested acres—for the first time ever.

These statistics aren't just distressing for young farmers looking to till the land; they're also bad for business. They suggest that farm-to-table has not, in any fundamental way, reshaped the American landscape or reinvented how our food is grown and raised. The on-the-ground reality is that Big Food continues to get bigger, not smaller.

How do we overcome this odd duality: an exciting food revolution on the one hand, an entrenched status quo on the other?

※ ※ ※

One way is to consider what Glenn did next, and it's not what we might expect from the same old farm-to-table story. After pulling his corn from the shelves, he put his nose even closer to the grindstone.

"I was told as long as the temperature of the grains in the milling process never exceeded forty-five degrees, you couldn't taste the difference," Glenn told me. Not one to trust conventional wisdom, he tried a batch milled at thirty degrees to test the difference. "Huge difference! So I kept going: twenty-five degrees, then twenty, and each time I tasted the grits at a lower milling temperature, the flavor improved, dramatically."

It became clear that he needed a language to describe the quality of what he was selling and he needed a market that spoke that language. So he called chef Thomas Keller at The French Laundry in Napa Valley, widely considered one of the best restaurants in the United States. Glenn approached the conversation as if he were a boutique wine distributor selling a sommelier a limited selection of the very best of a vintage. When he began his pitch about his premium grits, Keller interrupted him.

"I can't sell grits," he said.

Glenn proposed artisanal polenta, and at that, Keller was interested. Glenn promised to send some fresh-milled, organic polenta from corn seed stock that originated with Native American tribes in the Northeast.

"He agreed to try it," Glenn said, "which is when I knew I had the sale. Because once chefs try it, once they cook it and taste it, it's sold. A chef like Thomas Keller has a vetting process that relies on his tongue. It's the final word."

Glenn was right. A week later, it was on The French Laundry's menu. And within a few months, other chefs from around the country were requesting the polenta.

Which is where the story could have ended, but Glenn saw an opportunity. Utilizing fresh, low temperature–milled corn as a gateway drug, could he subtly encourage chefs—with their obsessive, pit bull–like allegiance to superior flavors—to drive an entire business and help build a cuisine?

Glenn dug deeper. He worked closely with his chef clients, educating them on how best to retain flavor through soaking and cooking the grains at lower temperatures. And he introduced them to other crops like Carolina Gold rice, Abruzzi rye, and Red May wheat—not just the ingredients themselves, but also their long-forgotten culinary applications.

In other words, he became a kind of rabbi to chefs, and to farmers, too. They needed a little more convincing. As Glenn likes to say, farming confidently is about having neighbors—neighbors who share infrastructure costs like seed cleaning and storage and neighbors who save plenty of organic seed. "So I decided to become the neighbor," Glenn told me matter-of-factly.

Glenn routinely purchases equipment for new farmers and guarantees that Anson Mills will purchase everything harvested at above-market prices. And he gives farmers free seed, with no strings attached.

That support network—along with the built-in market of chefs and educated home cooks—has spurred remarkable growth. Today it's not uncommon to see Anson Mills grains on menus around the country. They've been featured in food magazines and in cookbook recipes. Glenn's heritage seeds, soil-supporting grains, and fresh milling are seeping into everyday American food culture—and onto *refrigerated* market shelves—slowly, but inexorably.

* * *

Whether the bird lives or dies, it's in your hands. Is it fair to ask: should the rabbi have tried to argue more strenuously for the bird's freedom?

Because that certainly crossed my mind. As rabbis themselves have been known to ask: could more have been done? The troublemaker might have been warned of the consequences of his actions and the weight he would feel in taking a life. The rabbi might have pointed a finger—*Let the bird live!*—and in doing so, illuminated exactly what was at stake.

It wasn't until I got to know Glenn's story that I understood the rabbi's lesson as subtler and more lasting. It's about encouraging an ethos. It's about creating a culture in which the bird lives, rather than forcing the choice. It's about something very simple: Can people choose for themselves? Can we feel the weight of our decisions without anyone pointing a finger? Can we reach a point in our thinking—and our eating—where we no longer need to be told what to do?

If there's a moral to Glenn's story, it's to spend less time moralizing. The countercuisine movement of the 1960s and early 1970s was filled with dogma and virtuousness. "Don't eat white; eat right; and fight"; "Everything is connected"; and so forth. But very little of it tasted good, and it didn't last.

Glenn's lesson is to invest in a full farming system that doesn't rely on dogma or dictates. It is built on the conviction of good flavor, carried through from seed to soil to mill to kitchen. (After all, you can't have one without the other.) And it has created a community, a culture, and a cuisine around itself.

Glenn once tried to make sense of what Anson Mills had become. "Fifty years from now, that's when my work starts having some kind of meaning. And if I drop dead this instant, it carries on because it's out there now. It's happening at the speed of light."

No, he isn't a rabbi, a philosopher, or a sage. But he has built something that lives.

Now it's in your hands.

Dan Barber is the chef and co-owner of Blue Hill and Blue Hill at Stone Barns and the author of *The Third Plate: Field Notes on the Future of Food*. He has received multiple James Beard awards, including Best Chef: New York City (2006) and the country's Outstanding Chef (2009). In 2009 he was named one of *Time* magazine's one hundred most influential people in the world.

WILL HARRIS

I graduated from the University of Georgia's College of Agriculture in 1976. I begin this letter with that fact to make it clear that this was not written by a journalist; it was written by a farmer. What this writing may lack in polish is compensated for by authenticity.

In the 150 years that my family has worked our farm, we have come full circle in our production practices. The first two generations farmed with their focus on the land and the animals and the people. They farmed in cooperation with nature. My father began the process of industrializing, centralizing, and commoditizing the operation. I took this process to the highest possible level. Now my children and I are practicing the Savory method of Holistic Management and returning this farm to the holistic practices of my great-grandfather.

The industrialization, centralization, and commoditization were done for noble causes: they were meant to make food cheap and abundant and safe from transmitting acute illnesses. The changes made by the last several generations were wildly successful in accomplishing these objectives, but they brought about horrible unintended consequences. They damaged the welfare of our livestock, degraded our lands and waters, and impoverished rural America.

A small percentage of today's consuming public has taken note of these three tragic consequences and has been disgusted by them. These consumers have studied our food production system and have made lifestyle choices about the farm practices that they are willing to support with their food dollars. This consumer movement has empowered a small number of farmers to make meaningful changes in how we run our farms.

The farmers who are innovating to meet the growing demand for humanely, fairly, and sustainably produced foods are not making—and will not make—sweeping changes to the way America farms. These changes are small and incremental, as they should be. We have been in the industrialization, centralization, and commoditization mode for almost seventy years. Change to a movement this large will be slow, and it will never be complete.

When I was a young cattleman, anyone who focused on animal welfare was ridiculed. Today large, multinational agricultural companies greenwash their products in an effort to confuse consumers. The niche of the public that is focusing on a kinder and gentler agriculture continues to grow. To borrow from Gandhi: First they laugh at you. Then they fight you. Then you win.

Transitioning an industrialized, centralized, and commoditized farm to a farm that is focused on animal welfare, environmental sustainability, and fairness to all of the people involved is difficult. It is the hardest damn thing that I have ever done. But it is also the best damn thing that I have ever done.

Good luck. You will need it.

Will Harris is the fourth generation of the Harris family to farm White Oak Pastures in Bluffton, Georgia. He and his 120 employees pasture raise and hand butcher five red-meat species and five poultry species and produce organic vegetables and pastured eggs.

ANNA LAPPÉ

When I was in graduate school at Columbia University in the late 1990s studying economic development, our textbooks and lecturers delivered sermons on paths of progress. We learned about countries climbing so-called ladders of development, defined as moving from agrarian economies to industrial ones. We learned about the International Monetary Fund and World Bank loan protocols to promote such industrialization and about "economic miracles" like South Korea. In those stories, there was no place for a farmer.

But those lecture hall lessons were soon contradicted by what I would see on the ground and witness over the more than ten years since. For, alongside my graduate coursework, I was researching a book I would end up cowriting with my mother, Frances Moore Lappé. Together, we traveled to India, Bangladesh, Poland, Kenya, France, Brazil, and beyond. In each place, we connected with farmers and activists who were addressing the root causes of hunger and poverty. In remote villages and bustling city halls, on farm fields and in thriving economic cooperatives, what we saw was clear: farmers *were* the miracle. At the center of the community-based solutions we were documenting were farmers—farmers getting off the chemical treadmill; farmers knitting together productivity with biodiversity preservation; farmers protecting land, air, and water with ecological practices. In community after community, we saw the vital link between healthy people, healthy economies, and healthy farms—an epiphany that really shouldn't have been much of one.

In Kenya, we met women in the Green Belt Movement trained in agroforestry techniques who were bringing green to thousands of villages nearly consumed by desert; they were replanting indigenous trees whose root systems promoted soil health, prevented erosion, and protected watersheds. We met these "barefoot foresters," as they called themselves, who showed us their organic techniques for growing kitchen gardens of diverse, delicious, and nutritious foods. All of this flew in the face of a decades-old development paradigm that had pushed crops for export, such as coffee or cut flowers. These commodities did nothing to provide sustenance to the people of Kenya, and often, once the chemicals and other inputs were paid for, did little to provide income, either. Indeed, these practices so upset the status quo and the collusion between the government and chemical corporations that we met organic-farming educators who had been threatened with arrest for daring to teach agroecology.

In Poland, we connected with a farmer-to-farmer network protecting the Polish countryside still dotted with millions of small farmers. (At the time, there were as many farmers in a country about the size of Colorado as there were in the entire United States.) The farmers' network promoted organic practices and Europe-wide education, hosting tours of farms for their Western neighbors to demonstrate the vital role small-scale farms played in combating mounting European Union pressure to consolidate, industrialize, and open their doors to Tyson, Smithfield, and other multinational food conglomerates.

In India, we traveled high into the Himalayas to meet with farmers who were training villagers to become independent from chemicals—chemicals that had undermined soil health and led to chronic illnesses and even, at times, acute pesticide poisonings. These farmers were saving and replanting indigenous varietals, many of which were proving to be drought- and flood-resilient.

In country after country, I saw a new story line taking shape: emerging movements were revealing the negative externalities—as they would have put it in my economics courses—of agricultural industrialization and showing the power of ecological farming to promote well-being.

A few years later, while researching my third book, I decided to travel to the one place that had been presented in graduate school as the biggest miracle of all: South Korea, a country whose population had shifted from nearly 75 percent in agriculture in 1963 to just 21 percent only twenty-five years later. In my academic courses, the nation was held up as a success story of industrialization. But the people I met in South Korea—farmer and consumer advocates who were promoting sustainable farming in opposition to the government's endorsement of large-scale industrial agriculture—shared a different perspective. For these advocates, the "miracle" was not much of one. They were not longing to go back to the struggles of an agrarian past, but they were not excited about moving headlong into an industrialized future, either. These activists were fighting against corporate control of the food chain and promoting ecologically oriented supply chains, protecting indigenous foods, and building powerful consumer-farmer alliances. (One consumer co-op I met with had more than two hundred thousand members.) They were arguing that a healthy and sustainable nation needs a strong national farming movement, one that promotes ecological practices, keeps farmers on the land, and connects with urban consumers.

They were activists like the women who founded the Korean Women's Peasant Association in 1989. Sitting in their offices, I talked with movement leaders and heard about their connection with La Via Campesina, a global peasant movement founded in 1993. The association's office was piled high with fliers and strung with banners—evidence of past demonstrations against international trade agreements benefiting multinationals.

It was moving to hear these activists share their passion for this work, but the stakes only became real to me when I met the daughter of Lee Kyung Hae. She quietly introduced herself; it took a moment for me to grasp the significance. Her father had been the leader of the Federation of Farmers and Fishermen of Korea, who had helped to organize protests against the World Trade Organization to show how its policies benefit multinational corporations at the expense of farmers everywhere, including his members. At the protests against the World Trade Organization's 2003 meeting in Cancún, Mexico, Lee had climbed atop a police barricade and, while international news cameras rolled, committed suicide by stabbing himself—an act of ultimate sacrifice.

Meeting Lee Kyung Hae's daughter was perhaps the starkest reminder that for millions around the world, these are not academic debates about the role of farmers in an increasingly industrialized society: the struggle to protect farming as an honored way of life is literally a struggle over life and death. As we now know, for those small-scale farmers pushed off the land, industrialization has not led to "a smooth transition to the formal urban economy," but to "a highly precarious existence on the economic margins," as the *Guardian*'s George Monbiot puts it.

It's been more than six years since I traveled to South Korea, but I think about the trip often. I think about how far we've come—and how much more there still is to do. La Via Campesina now has active members in seventy-three countries, together representing more than two hundred million farmers worldwide. Yet farmers in nation after nation are still struggling to preserve their rights to save and share seeds from multinational corporations and to protect their land from land grabs for industrial operations.

Here at home, I see a reverence for farmers emerging anew. It comes, in part, with proximity: to know a farmer is to love a farmer. Thanks to efforts across the country, urban farms and community gardens are sprouting up from West Oakland to Detroit to Baltimore, facilitating just those connections. The US Department of Agriculture even has a Know Your Farmer, Know Your Food program now. This new attitude is also seen in the number of people farming for the first time: the fastest-growing group of new farmers and ranchers consists of those under age thirty-five. Young people are connecting with farming in other ways too, through groups like Real Food Challenge, FoodCorps, the National Young Farmers Coalition, and others. Universities and colleges are creating new food and farming-related courses, and food studies programs are emerging on campuses nationwide; more and more campuses are host to functioning farms.

The community-supported agriculture movement, started in the United States in 1986, is also giving tens of thousands of people a sense of reverence for farmers in a whole new way. When mothers like me can give children their first taste of blueberries and peaches, kale and sweet potatoes, beets and squash grown on an organic farm less than two hours from their Brooklyn walk-up apartment, that's reverence. When we can raise our children on farm-fresh, chemical-free food, that's reverence. When we see our children's bodies growing strong thanks to the food they eat, that's reverence.

I remember scratching my head in those graduate courses so many years ago when we were taught that farmers were a rung in a ladder to move beyond; when we were taught doctrines like comparative advantage that were simplified down to: If other countries can grow carrots more efficiently, why should anyone ever grow carrots here? I've come to see clearly now what those doctrines miss: farmers are the beating heart of a place. Farmers protect land and water, preserve cultural traditions, nourish communities, promote health and well-being. Farmers keep alive the very tastes of a culture. Farmers connect us with the earth and with the seasons. Farmers help balance the natural cycles so dear to life: carbon, nitrogen, water, and more.

When I get unsettled about the future, I need only think about the millions of people who wake up before the sun to dig their hands in the dirt to provide for the rest of us—and I experience that reverence anew.

Anna Lappé is a national best-selling author; the cofounder of the Small Planet Institute; and the director of Real Food Media, a collaborative initiative to engage the public in conversations about food, farming, and sustainability. She lives in the San Francisco Bay Area, where she and her family help organize a fish and seafood CSA and are members of a local vegetable and fruit farm.

JOEL SALATIN

=====

Here is what I'd want a farm mentor to tell me if I were a young person with visions of farming dancing in my head.

1. Create a working landscape. Because of civilization's track record of abusing the environment, many farmer wannabes are afraid to adjust the landscape. The radical environmental movement, with this abuse-legacy guilt, often promotes the notion that the only way to interact responsibly with the land is to get the humans off it. The best and highest use is to lock it up in parks, wilderness areas, national forests—what I call environmentalism by abandonment.

But I would suggest that the human's large brain and mechanical prowess (opposable thumbs) exist to interact with nature, to caress our ecological umbilical, to humbly exercise the ecology. Doing so stimulates more solar conversion into biomass than would be possible if the land were left untouched. Indeed, the difference between a farm and any other piece of property is what a farmer—the person—brings to the landscape. Absent the farmer, the land could be anything from a condominium to a national park.

Don't be afraid to carve in a road, build a pond, excavate a swale, install a root cellar, or construct a building. I call this participatory environmentalism—bringing healing and redemptive capacity to the landscape. The human is the most efficacious destroyer and the most efficacious healer; it all depends on how we implement our intellectual and mechanical gifts.

You can't work on a landscape unless you have access. You can't grow things if you don't have water. You can't process things unless you have infrastructure. Farms are not wilderness areas. They should be far more productive, be more diversified, and offer more value to the commons. Indeed, if our farms are places of innovation and activity, they'll be wilder than designated wild places.

Before you recoil in horror from my landscape aggressiveness, realize that I'm not calling for full-scale landscape destruction. But in true permaculture fashion, some rearrangement can make worlds of difference in daily efficiency and opportunity. A high pond excavated into a valley provides both flood control and a water supply in times of drought. And it provides a whole new riparian habitat that didn't exist before. To assume that every rock, every tree, every topographical twist and turn is in the best place because that's the way nature's last epochal event left it is foolish.

Go ahead and massage the landscape with refinement and ingenuity. It'll thank you for the treatment if you do it well.

2. Create eclectic awareness in your life. Too many farmers become insular in their lives, reading only their own orthodox materials. If you're a chemical farmer, read some nonchemical stuff; if you're a greenie farmer, read some chemical stuff. It's important to know what the enemy thinks.

Read and visit widely. Attend both sustainable agriculture seminars and government/corporate/agribusiness-sponsored ones. Have enough self-respect to make sure you're aware of trends, movements, and current events. Read liberal and conservative news sources; business, history, religion. All of this creates a renaissance persona that can stand toe-to-toe with any Fortune 500 executive. Get a nice suit and wear it; don't see yourself as a blown-in hayseed. View yourself as a modern Jeffersonian intellectual agrarian. What's on your bookshelf? How many hours a week do you read? Readers are leaders. Cultivate friendships across disciplines, politics, and religion. Entertain guests often; that's a cheap way to receive cosmopolitan information without having to travel.

It's easy to embrace things like permaculture, remineralization, biodynamics, holistic management. But don't be cultish; keep learning what others are saying and expose yourself to many different kinds of ideas. That way you'll make better decisions, and you'll be a more interesting, more attractive person. Farmers too often are known as hermit curmudgeons. We need to lead by example. Join a theater group. Take public speaking lessons. Be a storyteller.

3. Cultivate a can-do entrepreneurial spirit. Stay away from government grants, bureaucrats, and regulatory agencies. Surround yourself with positive thinkers and people who encourage innovation and weirdness.

Some would argue that farming is one of the loneliest and hardest vocations. Stay away from folks who say that; they'll beat you down emotionally and spiritually. Find and befriend people who love new ideas, even crazy ones. People who can enjoy brainstorming without passing judgment are catalysts for success.

This means you'll probably limit your time spent with other farmers—even your neighbors. All my life, my support group has been my farm customers. The neighbors think I'm a lunatic Typhoid Mary bioterrorist because they've drunk the Kool-Aid of industrial/chemical orthodoxy. They're toxic. Wave "hi" to them and enjoy cursory conversations, but don't immerse yourself in their fraternities or whining sessions.

Find people who are successful in their own right and excited about your dreams. Read positive books. Listen to motivational tapes. "I can" is far harder to do than "I can't." "Can't" is easy; anybody can do "can't." Only winners do "I can."

4. Live frugally. Many a new farmer gets derailed with a nice house, nice truck, and nice tractor. Those things may come someday, and I hope they do, but you earn those things by going through farming boot camp. You earn your stripes.

That means you live in a camper or yurt or tent or tree house initially while you get your farm up and running. You eat, breathe, and sleep your farm. Live simply so you can simply survive initially. My wife, Teresa, and I remodeled a farmhouse attic and lived there for our first seven years; we called it our penthouse. If we didn't grow it, we didn't eat it. Never had a TV; still don't. Never went out to eat. I've been to about four movies in my lifetime. Who needs Hollywood?

We drove a $50 car for our first two years of marriage and then sold it for $75 in parts. In our first twenty years of marriage, we didn't spend $10,000 total on cars. A customer gave us one for $1; we drove it for two years. We bought another one from Teresa's grandmother for $550 and drove it for two years. My dad gutted a 1957 four-door Plymouth, and that was our pickup when I was a kid. No seats and no doors; it made a big room to haul around kids (both people and animal varieties), calves, hay, and tools. Multiple use.

Stay home. No Little League; no ballet; no swinging at the park. If you want a swing, make one on the farm for cheap entertainment. Go for picnics by the pond you built. Take the kids fishing with worms dug around the compost pile. A farm provides all the recreation, entertainment, and wonder you can imagine. The kids won't care if their beds are in a rusty camper if their lives are surrounded by the awe of living simply with nature. If that's not appealing, then go live in the city.

5. Assemble a team. The various gifts and talents required for a successful farm business do not all grow on one pair of legs. Assess your strengths and weaknesses, and then focus on spending time where you're strong and finding someone else to do the things that are problematic. Believe it or not, somebody out there is waking up this morning passionate to do the thing you detest. Find that person and form a team.

Answer the question "If money and time were not an issue tomorrow, what would I do?" Now create a plan to spend more time finding the answer to that question.

Here is another helpful exercise: "What are you good at? What do you know? What do you enjoy?" Where those three universes intersect is the sweet spot for your success. Many times, we fritter away most of our time struggling with things we don't like or aren't good at and fail to capitalize on areas of passion and proficiency. Life's too short to be squandered that way.

Lest you think I'm advising you to hire employees, I'm not. Plenty of people want to join exciting teams with sacred goals. If integrity food and healing landscapes aren't sacred enough, I don't know what is. Create commissions and autonomous fiefdoms through memorandums of understanding to assemble a team without employees. Let people design their own ventures, create their own incentives. Let them take risks and enjoy the rewards of success. These kinds of collaborations usually make math look like 1 + 1 = 3. Things add up faster that way.

Don't be afraid to bring other people onto your team if they carve out their own incentives and share risk. The farm will progress much faster when a pile of warm coals huddles together. If you're just one coal, you can burn out before you ever get a fire started.

6. Direct market. You've heard the old adage "The middleman makes all the profits." Well, if that's where the profits are, sign me up. The more hats you wear in the chain of custody from field to plate, the more resilient your farm business.

By loading more of your dollars into processing, marketing, and distribution, you spread your risks away from production. Weather, price, pestilence, disease—the four horsemen of the farm's apocalypse—affect production. They don't affect processing, marketing, and distribution. The drought doesn't wither the Wi-Fi access you have with your customers. The grasshoppers don't eat the rubber tires on your delivery vehicle. Fungus won't destroy your stainless-steel processing tables.

By wearing these complementary hats in the food system, you create far more daily variety for yourself, which makes life interesting—perhaps even wild. You can fully employ yourself, even on a small farm. Value-adding enables you to enjoy incremental gross margins that a commodities farmer can't capture.

If you own your customer, you'll own the sale. The closer you can take your farm products to the end user, the wider your income footprint. Often adding a commercial kitchen to a small farm is by far the most strategic thing to do, rather than growing more and more of the same low-valued product.

Fortunately, we live in a day when many customers want to connect with their farmers. Capitalize on that trend. And it's okay to charge customers for hayrides and infotainment opportunities. They love it.

7. **Build multiple enterprises.** One-thing businesses are extremely fragile. Modern industrial farming orthodoxy assumes that one-enterprise farms are the most efficient. But nature runs on multi-everything: species, ecosystems (riparian, forest, pastoral). Permaculture students learn early the value of stacking.

Synergistic and symbiotic complex relationships define natural systems and therefore should anchor our farming systems. On our farm, we follow the cows with the egg-mobiles because, in nature, birds sanitize behind herbivores. We move the cows to a new paddock every day because in nature, herbivores move constantly. We use pigs to aerate the compost—pig-aerators—because in nature, animals move things around, not machinery.

Interestingly, all of these systems reduce capital costs, energy costs, and labor costs. I'm convinced that not one single farm in the world—ours included—is fully leveraging its air, soil, and water. Every time I think we've completely capitalized on our resource base, along comes yet another possibility to capture more sunlight, use the water one more time, build soil even faster.

Nature has no waste streams. All waste is the feedstock for the next production niche. Think about the farm as a bunch of cycles rather than as a linear factory input-output model. Think about it as a giant solar energy reservoir, and see how little the leak can be.

This includes leveraging your customers. A loyal beef customer wants to buy other things; let her. If you don't produce enough variety, team up with other folks who share your values and offer to sell their farm products to your customer. The one-stop shop built the supermarket; you be the supermarket. The hardest part of marketing is finding the customer; once you have a customer, she wants to buy more things from your venue. Make it easy for her to do that, and you'll both be rewarded.

8. Conduct your gross-margin analysis. Either marry, birth, or hire someone who's good with numbers. If it's you, great. But many farmers love production records and despise accounting and financial analysis. If you don't know where you are, you don't know where you need to go. If you're going to discover the weak link in your business, you need to know where the money is going and where it's coming in. A stack of invoices and bank deposits at the end of the year tells you nothing.

On our farm, we have some two hundred financial categories so we can correctly attribute every dollar of income and expenditure. That way we can run gross margins on all the different enterprises. This has enabled us to terminate some and ramp up others.

Gross margins enable you to run different scenarios to establish marginal reaction: If we did this, what would it do to our bottom line? If we adjusted this, what would it do? If you don't categorize your accounting, you can never know the results of your decisions. Successful businesses—and farms are businesses—invest in good financial understanding. That's a big part of making good decisions.

9. Do time and motion studies. Businesses do this all the time, but for some reason, farmers often believe they have a special dispensation that entitles them to not be concerned about efficiency. Hogwash. The world doesn't owe you a profit.

How long does it take to gut a chicken? Put away a dozen eggs? Plant a foot of carrots? Harvest a pound of lettuce? The numbers should be on the tip of your tongue for the things you're growing and the procedures you're doing. Wear a stopwatch and time different procedures. This is how you establish the labor expense, and it bears heavily on how you price your products.

On our farm, we've established benchmarks for many procedures, and we share them with interns, who can then time themselves as the season progresses and measure their efficiency. Have you ever put your movement patterns on a piece of paper at the end of the day to see if you duplicated footsteps? Arrange your chores so you go loaded and come loaded. At our farm, we never carry only one bucket of anything; carry two. If you don't need two, you can leave the extra one for the next time. Duplicating steps on the farm is one of the biggest daily wastes of time.

Make lists. If you do something that wasn't on the list, put it on at the end of the day so you can mark it off. This snowballs your accomplishment and lifts you emotionally as well as making you efficient. On our farm, we make big project lists and filler lists (things that we can do in less than one hour). This way, if you have a few minutes, you don't have to stand there scratching your head trying to remember what that one little thing was that you needed to do.

10. Build a portable farm. Today the average age of a farmer is nearly sixty years old because when entry hurdles are so high, young people can't get in—then the old people can't get out. We're in for some interesting times in the next decade. According to agriculture demographics, in the next fifteen years, 50 percent of all of America's agricultural equity will change hands. That's unprecedented in any civilization. We're truly living in exciting times.

The biggest impediment to entry-level farming is land cost. But what if you don't have to own the land? What if the farm business is independent of land ownership? In such a case, the farm can be placed on any piece of land—owned, unowned, borrowed, squatted, whatever. If the land-access arrangement falls apart, you can pick up the farm and move it to another location.

When we divorce the land from the farm business capitalization, it completely changes the entry economics. On our farm, nearly all the infrastructure is portable. We lease ten properties and move the infrastructure from one place to another. We call this nook-and-cranny farming. Portable chicken shelters, egg-mobiles, brooders, pig shade structures, cow shade structures: they're all mobile, modular, and management intensive.

Our farm equity is in information, management, and customers rather than depreciable stationary infrastructure, equipment, or land. What's even better, portable infrastructure does not require building permits, setbacks, or licensing. What's not to love?

Based on my own experience and from effective models I've seen around the world, these are the threads of success common to thriving new farm start-ups. Farmers are viscerally engaged in creation stewardship—taking care of nature and growing great food—which is a wonderfully sacred mission. But the mission does not override the need for good business savvy and personal discipline. These threads work in every climate and every culture. Now hold your head high and be the most successful integrity farmer in the world.

Joel Salatin co-owns Polyface Farm with his family in Swoope, Virginia, producing pastured livestock and servicing six thousand families and fifty restaurants via relationship marketing. The author of ten books and a frequent conference speaker, he advocates aggressively for food-choice freedom and local food systems. The farm has an open-door, 24/7/365 policy to showcase regenerative agricultural methods.

BILL MCKIBBEN

Dear young farmer,

As an old eater, let me first say "thank you" for this food we are about to receive. The work you've chosen to do is important to me on three major occasions each day and at frequent intervals in between. Without you, I'd have low blood sugar and be cranky. My wife thanks you, too.

And having said "thank you," let me move to the major theme of my letter, which is: sorry.

For the ten thousand years or so in which humans have engaged in agriculture—ever since the overwhelming need for beer caused some of our ancestors to become sedentary (an ongoing development, actually) and grow barley—farmers could count on the essential predictability of our earth. We called this period the Holocene, and the benign climatic stability of this era coincided, not coincidentally, with the rise of human civilization.

That climatic stability was predicated on the abundance of the carbon dioxide molecule in the earth's atmosphere. It hovered right around 280 parts per million for almost the whole run of the Holocene, until, in the eighteenth century, some of our fellows discovered how to use first coal, and then oil and gas, to transform the planet. This carbon binge—the combustion of tens of millions of years' worth of former dinosaurs and ex-plankton in the course of a few decades—has by now raised the CO_2 concentration of the atmosphere past 400 parts per million, a figure headed steadily higher.

Because the molecular structure of CO_2 traps heat that would otherwise radiate out to space, the temperature is climbing steadily as well; it's already up almost two degrees Fahrenheit and again headed far higher. As it turns out, this will make your life far more difficult than it was for farmers before you. Warm air holds more water vapor than cold air does. Hence, in arid areas, we will see more drought—in fact, we already are seeing more. In 2012, the hottest year in American history, the heat and drought across the Great Plains prevented perhaps a quadrillion kernels of corn from fertilizing, an epic crop failure.

And since drops of water vapor stay in the atmosphere on average only about seven days, the drought in arid areas is matched by the rapid increase in flood in moist regions. My home state of Vermont saw its greatest rainfall ever recorded in 2011, and the downpour washed away not only bridges and roads but also many lovely river-bottom farms, where patiently built-up soil was replaced by rock and sand in a matter of minutes.

For the Great Plains and Vermont, you could substitute virtually any other farm region on Earth. California. The rice fields of the Irrawaddy Delta. Or, say, the Fertile Crescent of the Middle East, which suffered the worst drought in recorded history in the latter half of the last decade. It sent a million farmers off the land and into the cities of Syria, where, in turn, they helped destabilize an already fragile political situation. Partly as a result, we now have endless war in the region and a tsunami of refugees trying desperately to leave.

It's a nasty trick we've played on you. For a hundred generations, if you could grow corn in a certain field, it was a safe bet your granddaughter would be able to do the same. That's now a sucker's bet. Even the most basic human acts are called into question: scientists estimate that the rise in heat and humidity has already decreased people's ability to work outside by about 10 percent, a figure that will grow to 30 percent as the century progresses.

All of this, of course, makes your work all the more important. We currently have an agricultural system built for optimum conditions: those giant monocultures yield heavily when everything's perfect. But they're like racehorses; they break down easily. You're going to need to be a draft horse—your watchwords "stout" and "squat" and "sturdy." Built less for speed than for endurance. It was bad enough that Adam and Eve ate the damn apple, condemning us to raise our bread "by the sweat of our brow." Now, in the wake of our second, carbonic Fall, we're going to learn what sweat really looks like.

Tough as we've made things for you, there will nonetheless be benefits. You're going to once more be acknowledged—for the first time since Thomas Jefferson—as the most important of workers. Soon our habit of taking food for granted will begin to erode; eventually people will think of, say, hedge-fund managers with the disinterest they deserve. Young people will trade playing cards of heirloom beet growers and organic apiarists.

Maybe a lot more people will even say "sorry." And "thank you." And look at you with affection, uttering that most eternal, unceasing, and important of human questions: What's for dinner?

Bill McKibben published the first book for a general audience about climate change, *The End of Nature*, in 1989. He has written many more books, including *Deep Economy*, in part an early account of the rise of local food, and he is the founder of the global grassroots climate campaign, 350.org.

BEN BURKETT

It is a pleasure and an honor to write a letter to a young, inspiring, new, and beginning farmer. I am sixty-five years old, and forty-five years ago, I was a new and beginning farmer myself. I have been blessed to be a fourth-generation family farmer and to have farmed land that has been in our family for more than 120 years.

Those individuals who desire to become farmers live very good, wholesome lives. Dedication, honesty, and the ability to be hardworking and long-suffering are just a few of the character traits necessary, along with the patience to deal with the weather, markets, labor, bankers, and government, which are just a few of the elements you will experience. Beginning farmers are not blessed with land, equipment, and knowledge of farming. But if you are willing to work hard, you can overcome these obstacles and develop a sound farming operation.

The ability to produce food and fiber for other people is a gift and a privilege—to know that you have planted a seed, nurtured it, and watered it until harvest. Someone, somewhere, will enjoy the fruits of your labor. There is new technology, but the same methods and practices still apply: turning the soil, planting the seed, knowing the season.

Farming is the oldest profession, and young people should be highly recognized for wanting to become farmers. New and beginning farmers can be of any age. To be a successful farmer, one must have a true heart and loving spirit. Sometimes things will not go as you have planned. One must prepare for the unexpected at all times. Good times and bad times, good years and bad years. But most of all, farmers are always optimistic; they always believe that the next year will be a better year.

A mentor or veteran farmer will provide guidance and patience. Farming know-how is passed from generation to generation. Farming is not an individual effort; one must always remember that it takes a team effort to be successful. My grandfather once told me, "Never go to the field or into the woods by yourself." I have always enjoyed the company of others.

Whether you farm for a lifetime or for three years, remember: the land will always take care of you as long as you take care of it and pass it on.

Ben Burkett is a fourth-generation African American family farmer from Petal, Mississippi. He currently serves as president of the National Family Farm Coalition and is an active member of the Federation of Southern Cooperatives / Land Assistance Fund and the Indian Springs Farmers Cooperative Association.

AMY HALLORAN

I grew up in the country, but I thought of the outdoors as a place to play, not work. My dad grew more stories than vegetables, regaling us with tales of fighting critters as we would eat the one cucumber that survived.

This was in the 1970s in upstate New York. I rode my bike past fields and tractors without paying them a single inquisitive glance. At school, the fence went up to a cornfield, but we never talked about the crops that surrounded us. In fifth grade, everyone had to draw a combine, using a textbook picture as a model. Why didn't we go see how the farmers harvested and stored their corn? Education was for the indoors, for classrooms, not farms.

When I got a job running a farmers' market, I was chagrined by how little I knew about farmwork. I had worked in restaurants and co-ops, so I had experienced cooking, serving, and selling food, but beyond growing a few herbs, I had understood food mostly in terms of shopping and preparation. Noticing my ignorance, I started to consider the work of growing food, and I wondered about the prejudice I'd absorbed against farming. When did our culture start to ignore the work of growing food?

I don't have all the answers, but I am growing more aware of what we can do to correct our attitudes about food. As a writer, I hope to take readers beyond the simple commandment to know your farmer and toward an understanding of the dialogs that extend over time from farmer to farmer, hand to soil, plant to hand, and ear to mind—conversations between people and plants that are essential to the way we eat.

My son has been a key informant. One day I was making dinner, and Francis, age ten, took a stalk of yard-grown celery from the sink. We both remarked on its flavors, so bright and lively, as if what we'd grown contained a concentrate of the essence of celery that supermarket celeries couldn't give us (or had lost). Francis then began to muse about seeds and the ancient shift from foraging to farming.

My own brain had a muddy picture of how agriculture evolved. One day, some people were chasing animals off cliffs, and then—poof!—the next day, other people started keeping animals in pens and planting crops. I urged my son toward more immediate tasks, like setting the table.

Getting good food—growing it, freezing or canning it, and trying to figure out how to afford high-quality meat and dairy—took up much of my life. I didn't have room for more ideas. Francis, however, absorbed ideas like a sponge, especially ideas about plants. He carried around seed catalogs the way other boys carried comic books.

At that time, my understanding of the way we eat was based on shopping. People took fruits and vegetables from plants, or from a store. I didn't know boo about humanity's grand project of coaxing food from the earth, or where or when it had begun.

Not long after my son brought up the subject, a wheat breeder at Cornell University gave me a quick history lesson and introduced me to a radical notion: eating is a conversation with nature, and nature has a strong voice in what is said.

This may seem obvious, but it was a surprise to me. I was interviewing plant scientist Julie Dawson for an article about how bread builds community. Julie had just returned from France, where she was helping farmers breed and select wheat varieties that grew well and baked well.

She suggested that this work echoed that of early peoples as they began domesticating wheat and barley ten to twelve thousand years ago in the Fertile Crescent. Those original farmers were foragers studying the landscape for edibles. I imagined them, running their eyes and hands over wild grasses and choosing plants that had useful properties, like seed heads that stayed intact instead of shattering and dropping seeds to the ground.

"People don't think about everything that goes into getting wheat into the field," said Julie.

In a flash, bright and sharp as the late-afternoon sun, I saw farming as a long conversation among people, plants, and the environment. I saw a line of people and plants stretching backward and reaching forward, into the ground and toward each other. Green shoots reaching for the sun, our arms reaching for the food; until then, I'd thought that people steered our food system, but really, we are just a part of an elaborate cooperative network.

We are not separate, shopping for food in nature's store, but actors in a natural system whose other components, such as tiny fungi and heavy rainfalls, play equally important roles. The awareness humbled me. How had I missed that this was not just about us?

I couldn't picture what early farmers had in common with modern ones until Julie showed me the continuum. I began to see that the way we eat is the result of intersections between flora and fauna, each responding to the other in a mesh of soil, climate, and seasons. Food doesn't start when a seed is planted by a person.

I am going on and on about this because I can't believe how long it took me to understand it. I love cooking, and my family and friends chat about the Latin names of trees the way other people talk about sports. I am surrounded by opportunities to notice how reliant we are upon the natural world for the simple act of eating. If I couldn't see it, just imagine how blind the average person, someone who has no affection for the kitchen, is to this notion. How come?

My favorite place to look for answers is the nineteenth century. During those hundred years, the Industrial Revolution, urbanization, and the mechanization of farm equipment drastically changed the work and perceptions of farming. Writers such as Liberty Hyde Bailey give me insight into these perceptions. The first head of the agriculture school at Cornell, Bailey's approach to farmer education was instrumental in establishing the USDA Cooperative Extension System, the mechanism that delivered research from land-grant institutions to America's farmers and communities.

While the extension system developed into a one-way flow from authorities to farmers, Bailey actually envisioned a much more integrated enterprise. He solicited information from farmers whenever he could, seeking input on how best to serve their interests. He argued that a farmer's worth should not be measured in strictly fiscal terms, but in terms of other satisfactions as well. "The rain means something to humankind beyond better crops, greater stream flow, the cooling of the atmosphere, and the laying of dust. Rocks mean more than building materials. Trees mean more than timber, more even than shade and refreshment," he wrote. Farm folk meant more than their numbers, whether counting their population or the goods they supplied.

Farm productivity became the goal in the United States, unfortunately, and yields the sole measure of farmwork, squeezing a factory framework around a way of life.

Today people struggle to see around that framework and beyond the food labels that define our diets. We want more connection to our food, but knowing our farmer is not enough, and we can't just vote with our forks. We need to vote with our intimacies and attachments and visualize the processes that let us eat. We need to see that long line of people and plants, from the under-paid farmworkers who handle our fruits and vegetables and bring cows into the milking parlor, to the people who shift the focus of their farm operations to keep living on family land.

We need to look back thirty-two thousand years, more than twenty thousand years before the start date of farming in the Fertile Crescent, at the stone tool recently found in southern Italy. It contained residue of wild oats someone had crushed. Milling predates farming. I love that the long progression from foraging toward farming now includes evidence of people collecting wild oats instead of just sowing them. The image of that work reminds us that eating is hunting in nature for food. That is still true, even if we are stocking our kitchens from supermarkets; industry is doing the work of hunter-gatherers.

As a storyteller, my job is to show that lineage as best I can. I want to depict the texture and subject of a farmer's work and show how farmers and nature combine their best efforts. I am only beginning to understand how clover fixes nitrogen and why overwintering wheat seedlings suppresses weeds in spring. I observe and try to articulate the ways that farm life and our meals are stitched to the land.

I am navigating my own awe so I can help reveal the invisible. I watch the sky and try to name the kinds of clouds that belt the horizon, try to imagine what it's like to have the weather be your boss. I study the buildings and tools on a farm, so I can name each piece of equipment—grain dryer, seed cleaner, seed drill—and tell how it does its job. I keep track of the shades and the shapes I see. The better I know this world, the better I can describe that long line of plants and people who collaborate to feed us.

Amy Halloran lives with her family in upstate New York. She teaches writing and cooking classes and cooks for a community meals program. Her book, *The New Bread Basket: How the New Crop of Grain Growers, Plant Breeders, Millers, Maltsters, Bakers, Brewers, and Local Food Activists Are Redefining Our Daily Loaf*, grew out of her lifelong devotion to pancakes.

NEPHI CRAIG

I am delighted to be writing this letter to you today, because as you are a young farmer, so I was once a young chef—a White Mountain Apache chef with little to no encouragement or Native chef mentors. I understand the rarity of your youthful decision to pursue farming when other options in life abound. Let me tell you that your choice to enter the realm of agriculture is an extremely important one, and one that must affect you in a positive way. I recall being misunderstood by my family, friends, and other professionals in my field. I share that to prepare you, should you encounter a similar perception or misunderstanding of farming in your life.

When I began cooking about eighteen years ago, I began in culinary school, as most young people do. As a Native person, I learned right away that I had entered a very different world in professional cooking. As I got deeper into the culinary curriculum, I realized that there was absolutely no mention of Native American people in our studies. There were areas of study related to Mexico and South America, but nothing about Native American cooking. When I approached my chef instructors and asked, "Have you ever heard of Native American cuisine?" I received a dismissive answer: "I know you make fry bread; I know you boil stews." This was a significant moment, when I was met with a misconception about my people's culinary history.

Growing up among the White Mountain Apache and the Navajo, I had experienced a different reality than the one my chef instructor believed. Growing up, I had seen food as sacred, with philosophical connections to our entire way of life. None of this was known or acknowledged in a respectful way early in my cooking career. I realized that Native American people had been deliberately left out of the culinary history of North America, despite the fact that the rich agricultural and culinary foodways of modern American cuisine have been built on indigenous foodways. This seed of alienation became the seed idea for me to found the Native American Culinary Association, in an effort to provide authentic representation of Native peoples in American cooking and world gastronomy while supporting emerging Native culinary talent. At this point in my cooking career, I can confidently say that Native American cuisine is the foundational *terroir* of all American regional cuisines.

I encourage you to delve into the various histories of the regions in which you learn and hone your craft. All across the United States and the Americas, there are deep and culturally rich indigenous histories—stories from the land and of the people who have produced food from it for thousands of years—that can be learned and shared. Each indigenous group holds an intimate relationship with its ancestral landscape, and the farming methods it employs reflect a deep appreciation for their entire way of life.

Dry farming, for example, is utilized by the Navajo, Zuni, and Hopi tribes all across the Southwest and speaks to their agricultural intelligence, which was developed and passed down over thousands of years of evolution, allowing them to become sedentary agricultural peoples. My people, the White Mountain Apaches, engaged in strategic agriculture, contrary to the false notion that we were "nomadic hunter-gatherers." In tune with our landscape and seasons, we were able to plant corn in certain areas and leave those areas to follow other wild foods and animals at various elevations throughout our territory. Apaches would return to tend to the cornfields, and when the harvest time neared, we would have "harvest camps" to gather, process, and store our annual yield. Such farm crops would be coupled with wild foods that had been gathered and preserved all spring, summer, and fall to prepare for the coming winter. This diverse approach reflects the diversity of the White Mountain Apache landscape, where elevations range from eleven thousand feet in the mountains down to four thousand feet in the desert. These agricultural foodways were also supplemented by highly developed and intelligently planned trade routes that stretched from Mesoamerica through Mexico and into our region in Arizona. Many indigenous ways of knowing are still applicable today.

As you till the landscape and cultivate a brighter future for people, please remember that your work can be considered sacred. You, your hands, the soil, and the seeds you choose to sow are at a crossroads with the cosmos. The plants that you cultivate will teach you lessons: they will help you develop a profound understanding of our cosmological relationship to all existence and promote a healthy appreciation and respect for our food plants and animal relatives. Your work will enable you to become a land advocate, and your hard work in the field will allow you to stand on an honest platform of integrity and food security as you develop your agricultural voice.

I encourage you to build healthy relationships with mentors, while always building within yourself a desire and skill set that enables you to teach others in turn. I encourage you to always be humble, so that you can be in a state of perpetual learning. I encourage you to begin teaching today, right now; start with what you know best. As you teach your craft, teach with heart and humor, creating an environment of safety so that your students will maximize their learning potential. I encourage you to sing to your plants as you would sing to your children. I encourage you to delve into the realms of science, epidemiology, nutrition, photography, creative writing, and public health. I encourage you to develop your voice, because you will be a practitioner with an extremely valid perspective. And I encourage you to always view your work as part of the larger picture of American agriculture. Remember that indigenous peoples' foodways reflect their traditional roles as stewards and protectors of the landscape.

Your work is the work that will sustain our future. There will come a time when your fields will be viewed as the most critical outdoor learning spaces on the planet, as the entire world looks for solutions for feeding a growing population amid climate change and other adverse elements of our diverse global food system. As a Native person, I encourage you to look at your work as healing the landscape and to look at yourself as a healer who nurtures humanity: you promote maximum brain function by providing healthy, wholesome, and delicious foods.

Build yourself into a healthy and intelligent farmer. Develop your skills in a way that can enable you to be a teacher to other farmers, your neighbors, your community, and beyond, because your work touches every level of human life. Know that the skills you already possess can be taught, but your work ethic, respect for land and people, and sense of responsibility are inherent traits, and you must lead by example.

Our indigenous American landscape can teach you lessons, too. Build healthy and respectful relationships with Native peoples in your area and read some of the great indigenous literary and historical works; one in particular is *An Indigenous Peoples' History of the United States*, by Roxanne Dunbar-Ortiz, which details the Native American history that is not taught in schools and universities. This book demonstrates that we are in an age when Native peoples are able to tell their own histories, which include culinary histories.

I hope to hear about your developments and understanding of your own form of ancestral knowledge as you interact with seeds, soil, light, and our cosmological relationship with our tiny planet. I encourage you to share as much as you can and teach every day. In turn, I pledge to support you and work with you and other farmers who care for the earth and respect its peoples. I hope this book, of which my letter is a part, has inspired you to excel.

I am glad to know that you are reading this. I am humbled to be able to share my thoughts with you because as chefs, we have strong work ethics, just like farmers do, and without farmers, chefs like me cannot do our jobs. I am excited for your pathway as a farmer. Thank you for your valuable time and attention to these matters of vitality, seeds, soil, toil, and our planet.

Nephi Craig, a White Mountain Apache/Navajo executive chef, is the founder of the Native American Culinary Association, a network of Native cooks, chefs, scholars, farmers, and community members devoted to the development and preservation of Native American foodways. Over the past eighteen years, Chef Craig has cooked throughout Indian Country on and off reservations across the United States, as well as in London, Germany, Brazil, and Japan. He currently is the executive chef at the Sunrise Park Resort Hotel on the White Mountain Apache Tribe in Arizona.

WENDELL BERRY

As often before, my thoughts begin with the modern history of rural Kentucky, which in all of its regions has been deplorable. In my county, for example, as recently as the middle of the last century, every town was a thriving economic and social center. Now all of them are either dying or dead. If there is any concern about this in any of the state's institutions, I have yet to hear about it. The people in these towns and their tributary landscapes once were supported by their usefulness to one another. Now that mutual usefulness has been removed, and the people relate to one another increasingly as random particles.

To help in understanding this, I want to quote a few sentences of a letter written on June 22, 2013, by Anne Caudill. Anne is the widow of Harry Caudill. For many years she was involved in Harry's study of conditions in Eastern Kentucky and in his advocacy for that region. Since Harry's death, she has maintained on her own the long interest and devotion she once shared with Harry, and she is always worth listening to. She wrote:

> The *Lexington Herald-Leader* last Sunday…published a major piece on the effects of the current downturn in the coal industry…Perhaps the most telling statement quoted came from Karin Slone of Knott County whose husband lost his job in the mines…finally found a job in Alabama and the family had to leave their home. Karin said, "There should have been greater efforts to diversify the economy earlier."
>
> [Fifty] years ago and more Harry tried…everything he could think of to encourage diversity. My heart goes out to those families who yet again are being battered by a major slump in available jobs….Again they are not being exploited, but discarded.

This is a concise and useful description of what Anne rightly calls a tragedy, and "tragedy" rightly applies, not just to the present condition of Eastern Kentucky, but to the present condition of just about every part of rural Kentucky. The tragedy of Eastern Kentucky is the most dramatic and obvious because that region was so extensively and rapidly industrialized so early. The industrialization of other regions (mine, for example) began with the accelerated industrialization of agriculture after World War II, and it has accelerated increasingly ever since. The story of industrialization is the same story everywhere, and everywhere the result is ruin. Though it has developed at different rates of speed in different areas, that story is now pretty fully developed in all parts of our state.

To know clearly what industrialization is and means, we need to consider carefully some of the language of Anne Caudill's letter. We see first of all that she is speaking of a region whose economy is dependent upon "jobs." This word, as we now use it in political clichés such as "job creation," entirely dissociates the idea of work from any idea of calling or vocation or vocational choice. A "job" exists without reference to anybody in particular or any place in particular. If a person loses a "job" in Eastern Kentucky and finds a "job" in Alabama, then he has ceased to be "unemployed" and has become "employed," it does not matter who the person is or what or where the "job" is. "Employment" in a "job" completely satisfies the social aim of the industrial economy and its industrial government.

Perhaps there have always been "jobs" and "employees" to fill them. The point here is that the story of industrialization radically enlarges the number of both. It also enlarges the number of the unemployed and the unemployable. I can tell you confidently that the many owners of small farms, shops, and stores, and the self-employed craftspeople who were thriving in my county in 1945, did not think of their work as "a job." Most of those people, along with most skilled employees who worked in their home county or home town, have now been replaced by a few people working in large chain stores and by a few people using large machines and other human-replacing industrial technologies. Local economies, local communities, even local families, in which people lived and worked as members, have been broken. The people who once were members of mutually supportive memberships are now "human resources" in the "labor force," whose fate (to return to the language of Anne Caudill's letter) is either to be "exploited" by an employer or "discarded" by an employer when the economy falters or as soon as a machine or a chemical can perform their "job." The key word in Anne's letter is "discarded," which denotes exactly the meaning and the sorrow of our tragedy.

How can it be that the people of rural Kentucky can first become dependent upon officially favored industries, the "job-creating industries" that their politicians are always talking of "bringing in," and then by those industries be discarded? To answer that question, I need to refer again to Eastern Kentucky and something I learned there—or began consciously to learn there—nearly fifty years ago.

In the summer of 1965 I paid a visit of several days to my friend Gurney Norman, who was then a reporter for the *Hazard Herald*. At that time a formidable old man, Dan Gibson, armed with a .22 rifle, stopped a strip miner's bulldozer. The land Mr. Gibson was defending belonged to his stepson, who was serving with the Marines in Vietnam. Mr. Gibson's defiance and his arrest caused a considerable disturbance, and a crowd of troubled people gathered on a Friday night in the courthouse in Hindman. Gurney and I attended the meeting. That night Harry Caudill made a speech that recalled certain meetings in Philadelphia in the summer of 1776, for he spoke against the domestic successors of the British colonialists: "the mindless oafs who are destroying the world and the gleeful yahoos who abet them."

I am indebted to another speech of the same night. That speech was made by Leroy Martin, chairman of the Appalachian Group to Save the Land and the People. Mr. Martin bore witness to the significance of Dan Gibson's act, his loyalty, and his courage. He spoke impressively also of the forest that stood on the mountainside that Mr. Gibson had defended. He spoke the names of the trees. He reminded his hearers, many of whom were local people, that they knew the character and the value of such woodlands.

Three lines of thought have stayed with me pretty constantly from that time until now.

The first concerns the impossibility of measuring, understanding, or expressing either the ecological cost or the human heartbreak of the permanent destruction of any part of our only world.

The second consists of repeated returns to the impossibility, at least so far, of permanently stopping this permanent damage by confronting either actual machines or political machines. Dan Gibson's unlawful weapon was answered by the lawful weapons of thirteen state police, a sheriff, and two deputies. Our many attempts to confront the political machine that authorizes the industrial machinery have really not been answered at all. If money is speech, as our dominant politicians believe, then we may say that all our little speeches have been effectively answered by big money, which speaks powerfully though in whispers.

The third line of thought, the one I want to follow now, has to do with the hopefulness, and the correction, implied in the name of the Appalachian Group to Save the Land *and* the People. The name of that organization—and, if I have remembered it correctly, Leroy Martin's speech—assumed that we must not speak or think of the land alone or of the people alone, but always and only of both together. If we want to save the land, we must save the people who belong to the land. If we want to save the people, we must save the land the people belong to.

To understand the absolute rightness of that assumption, I believe, is to understand the work that we must do. The connection is necessary of course because it is inescapable. All of us who are living owe our lives directly to our connection to the land. I am not talking about the connection that is implied by such a term as "environmentalism." I am talking about the connection that we make economically, by work, by living, by making a living. This connection, as we see every day, is going to be either familiar, affectionate, and saving, or distant, uncaring, and destructive.

The loss of a saving connection between the land and the people begins and continues with the destruction of locally based household economies. This happens, whether in the United States after World War II or in present day China, by policies more or less forcibly moving people off the land. It happens also when the people remaining on the land are convinced by government or academic experts that they "can't afford" to produce anything for themselves, but must employ all their land and all their effort in making money with which to buy the things they need or can be persuaded to want. Leaders of industry, industrial politics, and industrial education decide, for example, that there are "too many farmers," and that the surplus would be "better off" working at urban "jobs." The movement of people off the land and into industry, away from local subsistence and into the economy of jobs and consumption, was one of our national projects after World War II, and it has succeeded.

This division between the land and the people has happened in all the regions of rural Kentucky, just as it has happened or is happening in rural places all over the world. The problem, invisible equally to liberals and conservatives, is that the forces that destroy the possibility of a saving connection between the land and the people destroy at the same time essential values and practices. The conversion of an enormous number of somewhat independent producers into entirely dependent consumers is a radical change that in many ways is immediately catastrophic. Without a saving connection to the land, people become useless to themselves and to one another except by the intervention of money. Everything they need must be bought. Things they cannot buy they do not have.

This great change is the subject of Harriette Arnow's novel *The Dollmaker*. In the early pages of this book we recognize its heroine, Gertie Nevels, as an entirely competent woman. Her competence does not come from any "success," political or social or economic. She is powerful because, within the circumstances of her agrarian life in the mountain community of Ballew, Kentucky, she is eminently practical. Among the varied resources of her native place, she is resourceful. She has, from her own strength and willingness and from her heritage of local knowledge, the means of doing whatever needs to be done. These are the means, for her, of being content in Ballew where she is at home. Her husband, Clovis, is not content or at home in Ballew. He is an off-and-on mechanic and coal hauler whose aspiration and frustration are embodied in a decrepit truck. This is during World War II. The world is changing, and people are being changed. Physically unfit for the draft, attracted to modern life and "big money," Clovis goes to Detroit and finds a job as a "machine repair man."

Gertie and their children follow him to the city where, to Gertie, the cars seem to be "driving themselves through a world not meant for people." They find that Clovis has rented a disheartening, small, thin-walled apartment, and is already in debt for a used car, a radio, and other things that he has bought on credit.

In these circumstances, Gertie's practical good sense is depreciated nearly to nothing, except for the meaning it gives to her grief. Back home, she had dreamed of buying, and had almost bought, a small farm that would have given greater efficacy to her abilities and greater scope to her will. As her drastically narrowed life in Detroit closes upon her, she thinks: "Free will, free will: only your own place on your own land brought free will." (And now we should notice that those who have lived in the saving way preferred by Gertie Nevels— and some have done so—are solvent still, and Detroit is bankrupt).

It is a small logical step from understanding that self-determination for an individual depends on "your own place on your own land" to understanding that self-determination for a community depends on the same thing: its home ground, and a reasonable measure of local initiative in the use of it. This gives us a standard for evaluating the influence of an "outside interest" upon a region or a community. It gives us a standard for evaluating the policy of "bringing in industry" and any industry that is brought in. Outside interests do not come in to a place to help the local people or to make common cause with the local community or to care responsibly for the local countryside. There is nothing at all to keep a brought-in industry in place when the place has become less inviting, less exploitable, or less profitable than another place.

We may not want to oppose any and all bringing in or coming in of industry, but localities and communities should insist upon dealing for themselves with any outside interest that proposes to come in. They should not permit themselves merely to be dealt *for* by state government or any other official body. This of course would require effective, unofficial local organizing, and I believe we are developing the ability to do that.

But the most effective means of local self-determination would be a well-developed local economy based upon the use and protection of local resources, including local human intelligence and skills. Local resources have little local value when they are industrially produced or extracted and shipped out. They become far more valuable when they are developed, produced, processed, and marketed by, and first of all to, the local people—when, that is, they support, and are supported by, a local economy. And here we realize that a local economy, supplying local needs so far as possible from local fields and woodlands, is necessarily diverse.

As things now stand, the land and people of rural Kentucky are not going to be saved by the state and the federal governments or any of their agencies and institutions. All of those great official forces are dedicated primarily to the perpetuation of the corporate economy, not to new life and livelihood in small Kentucky communities. We must not make of that a reason to give up our efforts for better politics, better policy, better representation, better official understanding of our problems and needs. But to quit *expecting* the help we need from government bureaus, university administrations, and the like will give us an increase of clarity and freedom. It will give us back the use of our own minds.

For the fact is that if the land and the people are ever to be saved, they will be saved by local people enacting together a proper respect for themselves and their places. They can do this only in ways that are neighborly, convivial, and generous, but also, and in the smallest details, practical and economic. How might they do this? I will offer a few suggestions:

1. We must reject the idea—promoted by politicians, commentators, and various experts—that the ultimate reality is political, and therefore that the ultimate solutions are political. If our project is to save the land and the people, the real work will have to be done locally. Obviously we could use political help, if we had it. Mostly, we don't have it. There is, even so, a lot that can be done without waiting on the politicians. It seems likely that politics will improve after the people have improved, not before. The "leaders" will have to be led.

2. We should accept help from the centers of power, wealth, and advice only *if*, by our standards, it is actually helpful. The aim of the corporations and their political and academic disciples is large, standardized industrial solutions to be applied everywhere. Our aim, to borrow language from John Todd, must be "elegant solutions predicated on the uniqueness of [every] place."

3. The ruling ideas of our present national or international economy are competition, consumption, globalism, corporate profitability, mechanical efficiency, technological change, upward mobility—and in all of them there is the implication of acceptable violence against the land and the people. We, on the contrary, must think again of reverence, humility, affection, familiarity, neighborliness, cooperation, thrift, appropriateness, local loyalty. These terms return us to the best of our heritage. They bring us home.

4. Though many of our worst problems are big, they do not necessarily have big solutions. Many of the needed changes will have to be made in individual lives, in families and households, and in local communities. And so we must understand the importance of scale, and learn to determine the scale that is right for our places and needs. Brought-in industries are likely to overwhelm small communities and local ecosystems because both the brought-in and the bringers-in ignore the issue of scale.

5. We must understand and reaffirm the importance of subsistence economies for families and communities.

6. For the sake of cultural continuity and community survival, we must reconsider the purpose, the worth, and the cost of education—especially of higher education, which too often leads away from home, and too often graduates its customers into unemployment or debt or both. When young people leave their college or university too much in debt to afford to come home, we need to think again. There can never be too much knowledge, but there certainly can be too much school.

7. Every community needs to learn how much of the local land is locally owned, and how much is available for local needs and uses.

8. Every community and region needs to know as exactly as possible the local need for local products.

9. There must be a local conversation about how best to meet that need, once it is known.

10. The high costs of industrial land-using technology encourage and often enforce land abuse. This technology is advertised as "labor-saving," but in fact it is people-replacing. The people, then, are gone or unemployed, the products of the land are taken by violence and exported, the land is wasted, and the streams are poisoned. For the sake of our home places and our own survival, we need many more skilled and careful people in the land-using economies. The problems of achieving this will be difficult, and probably they will have to be solved by unofficial people working at home. We can't expect a good land-based economy from people who wish above all to continue a land-destroying economy.

11. The people who do the actual work and take the most immediate risks in the land economies have almost always been the last to be considered and the poorest paid. And so we must do everything we can to develop associations of land owners and land users for the purpose of land use planning, but also of supply management and the maintenance of just prices. The nearest, most familiar model here in Kentucky is the federal tobacco program, which gave the same economic support to the small as to the large producers.

12. If we are interested in saving the land and the people of rural Kentucky, we will have to confront the issue of prejudice. Too many rural Kentuckians are prejudiced against themselves. They have been told and have believed that they are provincial, backward, ignorant, ugly, and thus not worthy to "stand in the way of progress," even when "progress" will destroy their land and their homes. It is hard to doubt that good places have been destroyed (as in the coal fields) or appropriated by hostile taking (as in Land Between the Lakes) because, in official judgment, nobody lived there but "hicks" or "hillbillies." But prejudice against other disfavored groups still is alive and well in rural Kentucky. This is isolating, weakening, and distracting. It reduces the supply of love to our needs and our work.

To end, I want to say how grateful I am to have this audience for this speech. I remember when there was no organization called (or *like*) Kentuckians for the Commonwealth, and so I know its worth. I am proud to be one of you. In speaking to you, I've felt that I could reach, beyond several false assumptions, toward our actual neighborhoods and the actual ground under our feet. If we keep faithful to our land and our people, both together, never apart, then we will always find the right work to do, and our long, necessary, difficult, happy effort will continue.

Wendell Berry is the author of more than fifty books of poetry, fiction, and essays. He was recently awarded the National Humanities Medal, the Cleanth Brooks Medal for Lifetime Achievement by the Fellowship of Southern Writers, and the Louis Bromfield Society Award. For more than forty years, he has lived and farmed with his wife, Tanya Berry, in Kentucky.

"Local Economies to Save the Land and the People" was originally published in Wendell Berry's 2015 collection of essays, *Our Only World*. He first delivered it as a speech for Kentuckians for the Commonwealth in Carrollton, Kentucky, on August 16, 2013.

ALICE WATERS

Dear young farmer,

I want to start by saying "thank you." Thank you for choosing to be a farmer and for choosing to take care of the planet. Thank you for dedicating yourself to feeding us all. And thank you, too, for being the inspiration for my restaurant—indeed, for my life's work. You are my partner in change.

Forty-four years ago, when I first opened Chez Panisse, I could never have imagined that my restaurant would be anything more than a small neighborhood place for my friends to gather and talk politics.

When I was nineteen years old, I spent a year in France. I can honestly say that that single year completely changed the course of my life. It woke me up somehow. I felt like I had never really tasted anything before. In France, I was introduced to what we might now call "slow food culture," but for the French, in the sixties, it was just a way of life. Every day, I walked through the beautiful street markets on my way to school and ate in the local restaurants. I tasted things I'd never eaten before, things that opened my senses and that kindled something in my mind. I vividly recall the first thing that drew my attention to the provenance of food: it was a bowl of tiny, jewel-like *fraises du bois*, foraged from a nearby wood. And then came watercress—a tangle of peppery, vivid-green leaves and stems. These things were unlike anything I had eaten before. Those first tastes sparked a lifelong search for ingredients.

But it was about so much more than food. At that time, students didn't have to pay to go to concerts; you could go to a museum for free; there were wonderful public parks and spaces open to all: it was the full cultural experience, with good food always at its core. When I returned to the United States, I started searching for that quality of life but couldn't find it.

Naively, I decided to open a restaurant so I could eat like that again. I must have thought the ingredients would just magically come to us. But they didn't, of course. We had to go out in search of them. Or try to grow them ourselves. In desperation, I smuggled mesclun seeds from France and planted my backyard as a salad garden. But it wasn't enough. A generous friend then lent us a piece of land, which we sowed with vegetables. It never occurred to us that we had no idea how to farm: pests destroyed the entire crop; it was a disaster. Still, it was our own failed attempts and a maniacal commitment to taste that led us to the feet of our local organic farmers.

It started with just a handful of farms, but we immediately recognized that we had found what we were searching for: real food. And once we became acquainted with the world of farming, we hungered to know more, to discover new farms, to meet new producers, to taste new products. Each of these farmers was growing something unique: blushed Sun Crest peaches from Mas Masumoto, say, or fiery rocket lettuces from Warren Weber. We decided to hire a full-time forager (it's possible we invented the post)—someone whose job consisted entirely of "truffling" out new special growers and farmers and backyard gardeners who might have something special, *really special*, to put on our menu. We permanently removed the middleman and committed ourselves to paying the real cost of the food directly to the farmers. Before long, our local producers came to know that we respected their work and would pay them generously for it. Over the last forty years, we have built loyal relationships with the more than eighty-five farms that supply us.

Having that beautiful produce to work with in the restaurant so completely changed the complexion of our cooking that we decided to celebrate our relationship with our farmers as much as possible. We began printing the names of the farms and ranches on the menu. They weren't just any old boysenberries; they were "Bob Cannard's boysenberries" from his idyllic Sonoma farm. These acknowledgments were not just a way to honor our most important collaborators, they were also an education for our customers. This way, if they loved a particular plum, they might be able to track down its grower in the farmers' market and become that farmer's regular supporter.

Fifteen years into the life of the restaurant, we began to feel the need to connect more deeply with a farmer and were looking for a farm of our own. We were incredibly fortunate that Bob Cannard, a gifted farmer, wanted to work with us alone. By committing to buying everything that he grew, we were able to guarantee his livelihood. In turn, he taught us to treasure the land; from him we learned about *real* nourishment, about the rhythms not just of the seasons but of the years. Sometimes the apples might be small and tart and best used in preserves; other years they might be plump and juicy and destined for galettes.

Bob even took back all of the compost scraps from the restaurant. Whoever was tasked with driving the compost up was also responsible for bringing a fresh cargo of produce back: scraps for treasure. This introduced everyone working at Chez Panisse to a different set of values in relationship to the land. The kitchen and dining room became vitally connected to what was happening in the field. We became extensions of each other—what Carlo Petrini, founder of the Slow Food movement, calls "coproducers."

Petrini also believes that farmers are the "intellectuals of the land." They have the practical experience and rarefied knowledge to choose just the right seeds for a particular place, to plant them in the most advantageous way, and then to tend the plants and bring them to their perfect moment of ripeness.

This is what taste is all about. And it is taste fundamentally that makes my work irresistible and your work vital. I always say that farming is at least 85 percent of cooking, because it is taste that will truly wake people up and bring them back to their senses and back to the land.

Alice Waters is a chef, food activist, and the founder and owner of Chez Panisse Restaurant in Berkeley, California. In 1995 she founded the Edible Schoolyard Project. She went on to conceive and help create the Yale Sustainable Food Project at Yale University and the Rome Sustainable Food Project at the American Academy in Rome. In 2015 she was awarded the National Humanities Medal by President Barack Obama. Waters is the author of fifteen books, including *New York Times* best sellers *The Art of Simple Food I* and *II* and *The Edible Schoolyard: A Universal Idea*.

ELIOT COLEMAN

Attention to detail. It really is that simple. Those three words are good advice for all businesses, but attention to detail is probably more important on the small, diversified farm than anywhere else. That's because of the incredible number of factors that come into play when you are working with the natural world and especially when growing a wide variety of crops and livestock, to boot.

For a quick idea of the level of attention needed, consider the numbers involved. Some small vegetable farms may grow thirty-five or more different crops. And to spread out the offerings, they may sow four or five cultivars of some of them. Successional harvests require numerous planting dates. Those dates are determined by keeping careful notes during previous years. In total, that amounts to hundreds of varied and possibly unique decisions about crop rotations, soil types, specific planting and harvest dates, labor requirements, storage and handling, and other factors. I have always felt that anyone running a successful small, diversified farm could move right in to the CEO chair of a medium-scale business and not miss a step.

So let's start at the beginning of your year. Did you order the seeds on time and in sufficient quantity? Did you find a substitute for that favorite eggplant that was back-ordered? How much should you plant of that new, untried tomato variety? Do you have flats and marker stakes? Are the seeds stored properly? Is there sufficient potting soil on hand? Have you tested the new batch with a few trial seeds to be sure it is mixed correctly? Has the greenhouse heater been serviced? When was the greenhouse plastic last replaced? Have you checked to see that the bottom heat controls keep the flats at the ideal temperature for germination? Do you have an accurate thermometer for that task? Do you have an alarm set up in case the power goes out or the heater malfunctions? And those are just a few of the considerations on day one.

If you are producing crops and livestock products, you need to be set up to sell them. I guarantee there will be marketing surprises every year for the unwary. Are any of your stores and restaurants expanding or have some gone out of business? Are there crops they want that you are not growing yet? Does the new produce manager at the co-op realize that you have traditionally supplied all their winter squash? Will you have enough delivery crates for that new account you just added?

Every fall by tradition at a neighborhood farmers' potluck, one of us will read aloud E. B. White's delightful essay "Memorandum." I recommend it. In paragraph after paragraph, White's list begins with, "Today I should," "I ought to finish," "First, though, I would have to," "I ought to get some," or "It just occurred to me," and ends with, "I see it is four o'clock already and almost dark, so I had better get going." We all laugh and clink glasses, reminded that the life we have chosen is complicated and multifunctional, with more features than most people can imagine.

But there is no joy in doing anything poorly. We get our satisfaction out of doing it well. That means keeping our eyes open, writing down observations, never taking anything for granted, and acknowledging the veracity of the old Chinese saying that "the best fertilizer for any farm is the footsteps of the farmer."

Eliot Coleman is a farmer and author of many books, including *The New Organic Grower, Four-Season Harvest*, and *The Winter Harvest Handbook*. His market garden in Harborside, Maine, sells fresh vegetables grown in unheated greenhouses all winter.

BRIAN RICHTER

My uncle Martin grew cotton on 160 acres in central Texas. Some of my fondest childhood memories are of the days I'd help Martin irrigate his farm. I'll never forget the pure boy-joy of lifting the boards on the headgates, releasing water from the canals onto the field. The gurgling sound of that freed water and the satisfaction of watching it gush out felt like freeing a bird from a cage.

I also clearly remember a visit from the local extension agent who came to Martin's farm to badger him about using less water. The agent didn't need to constantly remind Martin of the tragedy that had befallen many farmers and ranchers in the region only a few years earlier, in the mid-1950s. A brutal drought had left every hayfield barren, causing many Texas ranchers to push their cattle herds north into Oklahoma in a futile search for green grass. Many of them ended up in the poorhouse, including another uncle, Bill. I think the only thing more painful than Uncle Bill's broken bank account was a heart left broken by having to put down a herd it had taken years to build.

The extension agent had been trying to convince Martin to stop relying on the creek that flowed past the farm for his irrigation water because the creek was sure to dry up again the next time a drought came around. He urged Martin to invest in a new center-pivot sprinkler system that could run on groundwater. That groundwater, the agent asserted, was like a vast underground sea that would never run dry.

It wasn't until many years later that I finally came to understand Martin's reluctance to wean himself off of that creek. To Martin, irrigation was meditation. The spilling of canal water, the long walk around the field to check that every row and corner was getting wet, was ritual to him. Sprinkling water just wouldn't be the same.

As Martin put it to me in trying to explain his Germanic stubbornness, "Once you've cross-threaded the bolt, the nut just never goes on right again."

Martin lived long enough to see his and many neighboring farms buried under the asphalt of Interstate 35, constructed to connect the burgeoning cities of San Antonio, Austin, and Dallas-Fort Worth. The Grove, my father's family farm, so named for its magnificent cottonwood trees, exists only in our oral history.

It did not take long for those growing cities to learn a lesson known to the farmers of the region: water has its limits. Those cities were planted in a landscape in which most of the renewable water supply was already being consumed on farms, leaving very little to water suburban lawns or flush urban toilets. But the cities grabbed whatever water was left, leaving many rivers and creeks bone dry.

I still cannot stand on the Congress Avenue Bridge in the heart of downtown Austin and look down at the Colorado River without wondering whether anyone else in that city realizes that their river is but a fading ghost of the boldly flowing river it once was. Draining a river is not just a problem for fish: the heavy reliance of urban residents and farmers alike on nearly exhausted rivers like the Colorado places them all at risk of water shortage when drier years arrive. Crops and livestock die in the fields. Power plants can't generate electricity because there's not enough water to keep them cool.

The exhaustion of our renewable water supplies is by no means limited to Texas. Across the western United States, half of all rivers have lost more than half of their natural water flows to cities and farms, and a quarter of all rivers run with less than a quarter of their original flows. Globally, one-third of all rivers are depleted by more than three-quarters, either on a continual basis or at least during drier years.

In the United States, more than two-thirds of that drying is attributable to irrigated farming. Globally, it's more than 90 percent.

Tragically, as we've raided the water accounts of rivers, we have in many places also begun to spend down the water savings stuffed under the mattress of the land surface. Millions of groundwater wells have been drilled deep into underground aquifers, pumping them at rates that far exceed their natural recharge. Contrary to what Martin's extension agent believed in the 1950s, we now know that those underground seas are not limitless. Water levels in wells surrounding Martin's farm have been plummeting for decades, causing farmers to pay a lot more for the electricity needed to pump water from evergreater depths. From the Central Valley of California to the coastal plain of the Atlantic Seaboard, we are now sucking up water that accumulated underground during the last ice age. It will take thousands of years to replace this water, even if we turn off the pumps tomorrow.

The widespread depletion of river flows has had a devastating impact on fish and other aquatic life. One of my most jarring memories of Martin's farm was the day that I took a stroll downstream along the creek after we had begun irrigating. There were hundreds of sunfish and catfish flopping helplessly on the dried-up creek bed. It was a poignant lesson that water left in a river is not water wasted: it sustains the web of life that we ultimately all depend upon.

The cities and farms of Texas and other water-stressed areas from California and Colorado to Georgia and North Carolina, and farther afield to Syria, Australia, and India, have bumped up against the limits of available water supply, leading to intense competition and conflict—strains that will further increase with climate change. The news media have amplified these controversies with stories about farmers pointing fingers at urban residents and their profligate use of water on lawns and in swimming pools, while city dwellers spout statistics showing that farmers are the bigger water users.

As my Nature Conservancy colleague Laura Huffman has said, "We've created a circular firing squad."

We cannot go on this way. In the water crises of our country and other regions around the globe, many water pundits see only a dark horizon. I refuse to see it that way; as a young farmer, you should know that there are many options and opportunities for resolving water shortages and conflicts.

But we really need you to lead the way, for two big reasons.

One you might think of as an offense tactic. If irrigation farmers in water-stressed regions around the globe could find ways to save just 10 percent of the water they are using, it would free up a volume of water sufficient to double the water being used in all the world's cities.

Not that we want to do that. But you get the point. It means that farmers have the power to substantially ameliorate serious water shortage, which the World Economic Forum now ranks as the number-one risk to our global economy.

The other tactic is more for defense. Everyone knows that most of our renewable water supply is going to agriculture, and so when other water users run short, they're going to blame you. Look at the recriminations against farmers in California when the drought started to get really bad in 2015. You need to get this stink off your back. Simply saying that you need the water to grow everyone's food isn't cutting it anymore. They're going to have to be convinced that you are using water as efficiently as possible, that you're not wasting any.

This need to save water does not imply a need to lessen agricultural production. Evidence mounting from around the world has demonstrated that yields can be sustained or even increased while using less water. By using water more carefully, we can get more crop per drop.

❉ ❉ ❉

In this crisis of water, there is tremendous opportunity for you and your community of farmers. Here's the deal that needs to be struck.

You agree to do everything possible — using state-of-the-art technologies and best-available irrigation practices — to save water on your farm. And you agree to allow other water users to make use of the water you don't need, for instance, by transferring some portion of your water-use rights to others who need water. In exchange, you ask political leaders to reform the arcane and perverse laws and policies that make it difficult to save or share water. (There are many.) These regulatory impediments create too much uncertainty in water exchanges, and they confound and slow the process. You should also be fairly compensated for your trouble. That compensation should include any real costs borne to enable your water savings, as well as a tidy profit to incentivize your good behavior.

Such compensation is not fantasy or wishful thinking. Examples of such deal making are growing in number every year. In 2015 alone, water managers for the City of San Diego paid farmers in the Imperial Irrigation District of California more than $60 million to save water that can be transferred to the city. They plan to keep on doing that every year, for at least another decade. Those funds can then be used by farmers to pay off farm debt, acquire land, or make changes on their farms that they could only dream of previously. Community water trusts led by nongovernmental organizations such as mine are emerging to facilitate the exchange of water among users and to return some water to depleted rivers.

I wish that Uncle Martin could have had this kind of opportunity. It would have been fun to think of creative ways to save some water on his farm, and with Martin's business savvy, he would have traded that saved water to another user and banked a nest egg.

And, just maybe, I could have talked him into leaving a little more of the creek for the fish.

Brian Richter is the chief scientist for the Global Water Program of The Nature Conservancy, where, for more than twenty-five years, he has consulted on more than 120 water projects around the world. He teaches a course on water sustainability at the University of Virginia and is the author of *Chasing Water: A Guide for Moving from Scarcity to Sustainability* and, with Sandra Postel, of *Rivers for Life: Managing Water for People and Nature*.

MICHAEL POLLAN

Americans today are having a national conversation about food and agriculture that would have been impossible to imagine even a few short years ago. To many Americans it must sound like a brand-new conversation, with its bracing talk about the high price of cheap food, or the links between soil and health, or the impossibility of a society eating well and being in good health unless it also farms well.

But the national conversation unfolding around the subject of food and farming really began in the 1970s, with the work of writers like Wendell Berry, Frances Moore Lappé, Barry Commoner, and Joan Dye Gussow. All four of these writers are supreme dot-connectors, deeply skeptical of reductive science and far ahead not only in their grasp of the science of ecology but in their ability to think ecologically: to draw lines of connection between a hamburger and the price of oil, or between the vibrancy of life in the soil and the health of the plants, animals, and people eating from that soil.

I would argue that the conversation got underway in earnest in 1971, when Berry published an article in *The Last Whole Earth Catalog* introducing Americans to the work of Sir Albert Howard, the British agronomist whose thinking had deeply influenced Berry's own since he first came upon it in 1964. Indeed, much of Berry's thinking about agriculture can be read as an extended elaboration of Howard's master idea that farming should model itself on natural systems like forests and prairies, and that scientists, farmers, and medical researchers need to reconceive "the whole problem of health in soil, plant, animal, and man as one great subject." No single quotation appears more often in Berry's writing than that one, and with good reason: it is manifestly true (as even the most reductive scientists are coming to recognize) and, as a guide to thinking through so many of our problems, it is inexhaustible. That same year, 1971, Lappé published *Diet for a Small Planet*, which linked modern meat production (and in particular the feeding of grain to cattle) to the problems of world hunger and the environment. Later in the decade, Commoner implicated industrial agriculture in the energy crisis, showing us just how much oil we were eating when we ate from the industrial food chain; and Gussow explained to her nutritionist colleagues that the problem of dietary health could not be understood without reference to the problem of agriculture.

Looking back on this remarkably fertile body of work, which told us all we needed to know about the true cost of cheap food and the value of good farming, is to register two pangs of regret, one personal, the other more political: first, that as a young writer coming to these subjects a couple of decades later, I was rather less original than I had thought; and second, that as a society we failed to heed a warning that might have averted or at least mitigated the terrible predicament in which we now find ourselves.

For what would we give today to have back the "environmental crisis" that Berry wrote about so prophetically in the 1970s, a time still innocent of the problem of climate change? Or to have back the comparatively manageable public health problems of that period, before obesity and type 2 diabetes became "epidemic"? (Most experts date the obesity epidemic to the early 1980s.)

But history will show that we failed to take up the invitation to begin thinking ecologically. As soon as oil prices subsided and Jimmy Carter was rusticated to Plains, Georgia (along with his cardigan, thermostat, and solar panels), we went back to business—and agribusiness—as usual. In the mid-1980s Ronald Reagan removed Carter's solar panels from the roof of the White House, and the issues that the early wave of ecologically conscious food writers had raised were pushed to the margins of national politics and culture.

When I began writing about agriculture in the late '80s and '90s, I quickly figured out that no editor in Manhattan thought the subject timely or worthy of his or her attention, and that I would be better off avoiding the word entirely and talking instead about food, something people then still had some use for and cared about, yet oddly never thought to connect to the soil or the work of farmers.

It was during this period that I began reading Berry's work closely—avidly, in fact, because I found in it practical answers to questions I was struggling with in my garden. I had begun growing a little of my own food, not on a farm but in the backyard of a second home in the exurbs of New York, and had found myself completely ill prepared, especially when it came to the challenges posed by critters and weeds. An obedient child of Thoreau and

Emerson (both of whom mistakenly regarded weeds as emblems of wildness and gardens as declensions from nature), I honored the wild and didn't fence off my vegetables from the encroaching forest. I don't have to tell you how well that turned out. Thoreau did plant a bean field at Walden, but he couldn't square his love of nature with the need to defend his crop from weeds and birds, and eventually he gave up on agriculture. Thoreau went on to declare that "if it were proposed to me to dwell in the neighborhood of the most beautiful garden that ever human art contrived, or else of a dismal swamp, I should certainly decide for the swamp." With that slightly obnoxious declaration, American writing about nature all but turned its back on the domestic landscape. It's not at all surprising that we got better at conserving wilderness than at farming and gardening.

It was Wendell Berry who helped me solve my Thoreau problem, providing a sturdy bridge over the deep American divide between nature and culture. Using the farm rather than the wilderness as his text, Berry taught me I had a legitimate quarrel with nature—a lover's quarrel—and showed me how to conduct it without reaching for the heavy artillery. He relocated wildness from the woods "out there" (beyond the fence) to a handful of garden soil or the green shoot of a germinating pea, a necessary quality that could be not just conserved but cultivated. He marked out a path that led us back into nature, no longer as spectators but as full-fledged participants.

Obviously much more is at stake here than a garden fence. My Thoreau problem is another name for the problem of American environmentalism, which historically has had much more to say about leaving nature alone than about how we might use it well. To the extent that we're finally beginning to hear a new, more neighborly conversation between American environmentalists and American farmers, not to mention between urban eaters and rural food producers, Berry deserves much of the credit for getting it started with sentences like these:

> Why should conservationists have a positive interest in…farming? There are lots
> of reasons, but the plainest is: conservationists eat. To be interested in food but not
> in food production is clearly absurd. Urban conservationists may feel entitled to be
> unconcerned about food production because they are not farmers. But they can't be
> let off so easily, for they are all farming by proxy. They can eat only if land is farmed
> on their behalf by somebody somewhere in some fashion. If conservationists will

attempt to resume responsibility for their need to eat, they will be led back fairly directly to all their previous concerns for the welfare of nature.

—*Conservationist and Agrarian*, 2002

That we are all implicated in farming—that, in Berry's now-famous formulation, "eating is an agricultural act"—is perhaps his signal contribution to the rethinking of food and farming underway today. All those taking part in that conversation, whether in the White House or at the farmers' market, are deep in his debt.

Michael Pollan is the author of several best-selling books on food and farming, including *The Omnivore's Dilemma*, *In Defense of Food*, *Food Rules*, and, most recently, *Cooked*. He teaches journalism at the University of California, Berkeley.

This essay has been excerpted from Michael Pollan's introduction to Wendell Berry's book, *Bringing It to the Table: On Farming and Food.*

FRED KIRSCHENMANN

Dear young farmer,

You are a member of a growing number of millennials who want to farm. And I am so grateful. You are part of an incredible gift that comes to us all at time when we need you.

For the past several decades, we have been operating under the assumption, spread by the government, that we have too many farmers. In the 1970s, Secretary of Agriculture Earl Butz told farmers that they had to "get big or get out." So our farms got dramatically larger, and our farmers, on average, got significantly older. In addition, in commodity agriculture, we created a market infrastructure that demanded that these farmers operate on the single principle of maximum, efficient production for short-term economic return.

As a result, we now find ourselves in a situation in which one-third of US farmland is currently farmed by people who are over age sixty-five, the average cost of farmland is the highest it has ever been, and farmers are forced to operate by a single principle: produce as much as possible.

But what about the next generation? How can young farmers acquire an adequate amount of land, which in many regions has become very expensive, along with the necessary equipment, and continue to produce more in order to compete in our get-big-or-get-out culture? Even in the case of multigenerational farms, retiring farmers expect the assets of the farm to fund their retirement, while their children and grandchildren expect that the assets will be passed on to them to enable them to begin farming on their own.

Add to this the fact that an increasing number of investors are now interested in investing in farmland rather than the stock market, since they believe land is a more reliable bet. Naturally, that further drives up the value of farmland, making it even more difficult for young people to enter farming.

On the good-news side, evidence is emerging that when farmers can cooperate to add value to their production, brand their own products, and reduce their transaction costs, returns to the farm increase, making it more possible for the next generation to enter farming. The average age of farmers of such values-based farms is actually getting significantly younger, indicating that young people growing up in such enterprises now remain on the farm, rather than leaving.

Beginning farmers who want to produce food for people, rather than commodities for the mass market, operate on a much smaller scale and with smaller equipment than do commodity farms, and therefore are also having more success as they enter farming. The number of young farmers who produce for farmers' markets, community-supported agriculture, and Internet sales is growing rapidly.

Such innovative farming systems tend to be more complex and require more labor. Yet a new food culture is emerging that provides beginning farmers with more supportive opportunities. For many food customers, the goal of "fast, convenient, and cheap" is rapidly being replaced by the idea of "memory, romance, and trust." Rick Schnieders, the former head of Sysco and one of my fellow board members at Stone Barns Center, originally articulated that latter idea, noting that customers increasingly want food that tastes so good, they build a memory connection to it. They want food that comes out of good stories from the land: how farm workers are treated, how the environment is cared for, who the farmers are. These stories lead to more trusting relationships between grower and eater, and to more community-linked food systems where farmers become part of a regional food hub in which they, processors, and eaters together create a food system based on shared value.

Such shared-value relationships are now being recognized as essential to successful businesses. In 2011 Michael Porter and Mark Kramer, writing in the *Harvard Business Review*, warned that businesses could no longer operate by "the old playbook" in which businesses achieved success by marginalizing labor and raw material inputs and by externalizing social and environmental costs, all in the interest of maximizing financial returns. They point out that we are now rapidly reaching a point at which our labor and raw materials—our social and natural capital—are becoming so compromised and depleted that a new business model based on shared value is going to be essential in the future. In fact, we are already beginning to see a shift in the corporate food landscape, as a number of major US food companies are making incremental changes— from offering antibiotic-free meats to cage-free eggs and more local produce— because their customers are demanding it.

Such shifts are creating incredible new opportunities for the new generation of dedicated, agroecologically minded young farmers—like you. And such shifts will necessarily be grounded in a new food and farming ethic.

It was such an ethic, instilled in me by my father, that led me down my lifelong food and agriculture journey. My father and mother started farming on our land in North Dakota right after they got married, in 1930—the beginning of the Great Depression and the Dust Bowl, an extremely difficult time to be young farmers. But my father somehow understood, intuitively, that the tragedy of the Dust Bowl was not just about the weather (which most of his neighbors believed was the case) but also about the way farmers farmed. Core land stewardship values had been abandoned in the early 1900s in the interest of maximizing production; hence, much land was left exposed to the devastating drought and winds. As a result, my father became a radical advocate of taking care of the land.

My father took great interest in instilling land-stewardship values in me at a very young age—the same values that later attracted me to organic agriculture and an interest in restoring the health of soil.

It is now clear to me that as we face challenges such as the depletion of fossil fuels, minerals, and freshwater resources, as well as a more unstable climate, our heavily resource-dependent industrial farming system of the past century will need to be replaced by more regenerative, self-renewing, and self-regulating farming enterprises. Thankfully, so many young and beginning farmers like you already embrace this ethic; in fact, it may be the reason you are farming.

Many visionaries have understood the inherent importance of these principles: Sir Albert Howard, F. H. King, Liberty Hyde Bailey, Aldo Leopold, William Albrecht, Hans Jenny, Wes Jackson, and others provide inspiring and cogent ethical principles that can ground your work. As Leopold poignantly reminded us, land is "not a commodity belonging to us" but "a community to which we belong." He also insisted that enhancing "the capacity of the land for self-renewal" was a core principle of any land ethic.

Such a transition to a culture that values the land's health will be challenging, given our current culture of maximum, efficient production for short-term economic return; but it is possible and necessary, and in the long run, it will be essential to both the success, and the joyfulness, of the future of farming.

Such a transition is one that we all—farmers, food entrepreneurs, and eaters—have to engage in together, as food citizens, devoted to creating a viable, sustainable food system for our future and the future of our children and grandchildren.

Welcome aboard!

Fred Kirschenmann is president of the board of Stone Barns Center for Food and Agriculture and Distinguished Fellow at the Leopold Center for Sustainable Agriculture at Iowa State University, where he is also a professor in the Department of Religion and Philosophy. Since the 1970s he has managed his family's 1,800-acre certified-organic farm in south-central North Dakota, and he is the author of *Cultivating an Ecological Conscience: Essays from a Farmer Philosopher.*

NANCY VAIL and JERED LAWSON

———

Dear young farmer,

If there's one job in the world that offers the chance to save humanity on the planet, it's yours. No pressure.

Really, we're not kidding. But maybe you know that already, as it's why you picked up this book. You want to be part of the solution. You want to be living a purposeful life. You want your joy to be authentic, bubbling up from the satisfaction of a job well done. As poet Marge Piercy writes, "The pitcher cries for water to carry and a person for work that is real."

We can't think of another occupation that has such transformative potential. For what has caused our current global predicament is the fracturing of the very relationships that your job rebuilds: that of you to yourself, you to other people, and you to the earth.

At Pie Ranch, we look at our relationships through the lens of health and justice. What are your relationships like? Are you taking care of yourself? Do the environment and nonhuman life also have the health and justice they deserve? How about your nested communities, other people? It's easier to hurt a farmworker who picks tomatoes in Florida if you don't see how the tomato on your sandwich is linked to that person's life.

But you are a farmer who wants to be kind.

And that's where it gets exciting. It's simple, sort of, right? Just start growing food in a more healthful and just way near people who want to feed themselves well, especially people with limited access to such foods. Voilà! Shorten the supply chain. People to people. People to place. But you know that.

So what prevents a million more people like you from starting such relationship-based enterprises? Farming is hard work, food is undervalued, good land is hard to access, early-stage infrastructure can be costly, running a business that pays a living wage is difficult. And, oh yeah, we're up against corporate greed, ignorance, and fear.

So where is the hope? *Expecto patronum!* It lies in the fact that you are willing to make sacrifices to start a farm and restore relationships with people. Just recently at Stone Barns Center's Young Farmers Conference, a good 75 percent of the attendees were first-generation aspiring farmers. That means we are beginning again to build up a culture around farming, but this time with both the inherited knowledge and a new suite of values that can make farms agents of social change.

We also noticed that most of the attendees were white like the two of us. As farmers who want authentic change in the food system, we can't forget how white people have benefited materially—and perhaps suffered spiritually—from stolen lands and stolen peoples.

For us, it's helpful to remember: the plant is not bad, but the soil it's been growing in is toxic, so the plant takes up that toxicity into its being. Don't take it so personally, but do take responsibility. It is possible to rid the soil of toxins and grow healthier plants—and people too.

As two white, heterosexual, landowning, coexecutive directors of a nonprofit embedded in a capitalist society, we try our best to leverage power and privilege for social change while not repeating patterns of oppression. We are supremely imperfect and make mistakes, but we put our trust in knowing that transformation comes when nurturing a beloved community rooted in health and justice.

We listen to communities of color. We work with other white people to unlearn systemic racism. Our HomeSlice youth interns build community with other youth, informing our crop plans and programs. Our emerging farmers learn about #BLM (Black Lives Matter) alongside CEC (cation exchange capacity). Our elders, who form an intergenerational network of support, share their stories with our youth and hold our organization with love. Our partnership with the Amah Mutsun Tribal Band shows us how to weave together indigenous land management with modern organic practices. Our work with the Agricultural Justice Project guides us toward paying our workers living wages. Our work with large company and public school cafeterias supports scaling our approach to annual crop rotation with pastured animals—giving us a way to sequester carbon and to demonstrate how farms can become part of the solution to climate change. Our collaboration with land trusts and public agencies helps make land accessible and affordable—not just for us but also for other aspiring farmers in the area.

Remember, we all have indigenous roots, stories, and traditions that have been erased in our rush to assimilate with the dominant white culture. Somewhere in our DNA, those traditions are longing to be translated into the now: plunging hands into moist soil, giving thanks for the water, reaching for a hand in a dance. Knowing your history, honoring your ancestors, taking responsibility for the skin that contains your spirit—all this and more we must do as we engage the gears on the tractor, reach out to a CSA member, order cover-crop seed. The inner work transforms the outer work. Your evolution is inextricably connected to our collective evolution.

As activist and writer Grace Lee Boggs said, "You cannot change any society unless you take responsibility for it, unless you see yourself as belonging to it and responsible for changing it."

As Princess Leia said, "You're my only hope!"

Nancy Vail and **Jered Lawson** are cofounders and codirectors of Pie Ranch, a food and farming education center on the San Mateo coast in California. Pie Ranch cultivates a healthy and just food system from seed to table through food education, farmer training, and regional partnerships. Nancy and Jered live on the farm with their two children, Lucas and Rosa.

TEMPLE GRANDIN

When I was a child, I never would have imagined that I was destined for a career in agriculture.

My interest in beef cattle started in high school after I visited my aunt's ranch in Arizona. Up until the age of fifteen, I had always been an Easterner, and when I ventured west, I loved it.

From many conversations with people in various careers, I've been fascinated to learn that high school is a critical time for getting students introduced to a successful career path. A special high school teacher often opens the door to a career in fields as diverse as physics or agriculture. For students to become interested in something that can be turned into a career, they have to be exposed to it. When I was a bored, poorly motivated high school student, my science teacher sparked my interest in optical illusions. (I really did build the optical illusion room that was shown in the HBO movie about me.)

Years later, when I started working on cattle-handling facility design, my knowledge of optical illusions made me think about what cattle were seeing. I observed that they would often stop and look at shadows. At the time, nobody else ever thought to look at what cattle were seeing, and I really did get down in the chute to get a cow's-eye view. In the early 1970s, this was radical thinking.

It is essential for everybody who works in agriculture to reach out to students when they are still in high school. Keeping 4-H and National FFA Organization programs in high school is essential, and classes at places like Stone Barns Center can get a student interested in working with plants or animals.

I wish to thank the teachers who helped me: Mr. Bill Carlock, my science teacher, and Ann Bredeen at my aunt's ranch were mentors who guided me through a rocky road to adulthood.

Temple Grandin is a professor of animal science at Colorado State University. Some of her books are *Animals in Translation*, *Thinking in Pictures*, and *Improving Animal Welfare: A Practical Approach*.

WENDY MILLET

Physically, ecologically, and culturally, we are what we eat, and what we eat has never changed more rapidly and dramatically than it has over the past fifty years. These changes have had a profound effect on our health, our communities, and our planet. Yet, slowly but steadily, the lines we have relied on to help us divide and explain the complex world around us have blurred as modern science has grown more capable of seeing the truth that's been there all along: everything is connected.

Concepts such as local/global, soil/water, mind/gut, rural/urban, and politics/food have become less useful and descriptive as we see that all are inextricably connected; that something so seemingly trivial and small as the microorganisms in the dirt can affect the climate of the entire planet. This knowledge is at once empowering and humbling. If everything is an integral part of a complex whole, then humans are neither masters of nor slaves to nature. Rather, we *are* nature.

It has now fallen on your generation, more than any that has come before, to craft a food system that embraces this reality and shapes a future that no longer puts human needs at odds with human survival. I expect this responsibility in large part shaped your ambition to work with food and working landscapes, as it did for me. Agriculture over the next fifty years will be about so much more. It will be about soil, politics, wildlife, community, security, nutrition, climate, psychology, education, and justice. How we approach and care for the complex natural world that we inhabit—and that we are—is the most important question humans must answer, and so I'd like to share what I've learned in the hope that it will help you in your important work.

1. Production and conservation can be complementary. Even among sustainably minded food professionals, conservation and production are considered to be, at best, unrelated and, at worst, mutually exclusive. The false dichotomy that separates the two as distinct and opposing outcomes has been a significant drag on progress and innovation in both fields. In my years working on ranches in Wyoming and Montana and then later for The Nature Conservancy, it became apparent to me that the debate over which outcome should take precedence is unproductive and unnecessary, because when done properly, conservation and production can be mutually beneficial.

For those willing to look, the natural world provides us with answers to the very modern question "How can we feed the world and care for the land?" Ecosystems are tremendous exponential feedback loops that have evolved to take solar energy, generate biomass, and feed a tremendous biological diversity of plants and animals that cycle and synthesize nutrients and allow for even more biomass to grow. This incredible symbiosis has functioned for hundreds of millions of years—that is, until humans began insisting that nature do things our way.

Much of agriculture and conservation today operates on fairly simple but ultimately counterproductive principles. For conservation, the goal is often to get livestock out of nature; for agriculture, it is to get nature out of livestock. Fencing off our cherished lands for human uses only and feeding antibiotics to animals housed in factory farms have further interrupted the amazing symbiosis that exists between animals and the land, creating new and unnecessary problems for both.

Great opportunity awaits those who are willing to see past this false dichotomy. I've seen remarkable results firsthand when we look to nature as a guide for how to care for our lands and feed our communities. At TomKat Ranch, we are inspired by the relationship between large herds of ruminants and the grasslands they graze. In the past, large and dense herds of herbivores migrated over prairies, steppes, savannas, and pampas around the world. They grazed, trampled, and fertilized the grasses, and their manure fed the soil's microbial community and ultimately allowed for even more grass and soil to grow. This vibrant and stimulating herd movement was not only the most critical element in the health of the animals and the land but also the very thing missing in conservation and production today.

Our model at TomKat Ranch mimics this natural system by planning and choreographing a ranch-scale migration for our herd. Each year, we meticulously plan where and when the cattle ought to be grazed in order to accomplish our production and conservation goals. Then our skilled ranch staff and apprentices use low-stress animal herding and portable solar-powered electric fences to keep the herd where it needs to be each day.

This simple change has had tremendous positive effects on our land and cattle. We have watched as our herd and our lands have simultaneously improved, creating that iconic positive feedback loop that defines a healthy ecosystem. In just our first three years of planned grazing, we saw a near-tenfold increase in native and perennial grasses on the ranch. These grasses help to increase soil health and water retention, and they also provide our cattle with months of extra green grass, as deeper-rooting and well-adapted grasses keep growing long after their annual and imported cousins have given up.

The healthier grasslands and constant mini-migrations boost individual cattle performance as well. Herd health issues began disappearing, and our 100 percent grass-fed animals saw seasonal weight gains near corn-fed levels during the spring finishing season. And we have marveled as the ranch's resident wildlife population expanded, too. This win-win for conservation and production has become a critical hallmark for us, a sign that the ideas fueling our ranch management are working. When I hear that ranch staff have been bragging at the coffee shop in town about how many mountain lions call our ranch home, I know we are on the right track. They understand the importance of a healthy ecosystem that encompasses all of its parts, even predators that might be a threat to our cows.

Many in the conservation sphere are also beginning to realize that livestock can be a useful tool for achieving their goals. A lot of my time is spent talking with land trusts, conservation organizations, and conservation-minded private landowners about how planned grazing can revitalize the land. For those just entering the sustainable food profession, this blending of conservation and production is an incredibly fertile area in which to start a career. As more positive examples of blending conservation and production are documented, skilled, innovative, and forward-thinking managers and planners will be in high demand to help us realign our lands and our food system with the time-tested and abundant example that nature provides.

2. Manage diversity with diversity. While it is far easier than fighting nature, working *with* nature can be incredibly challenging because problems cannot be reduced to a single variable. Our modern minds prefer problems to be cut-and-dried and solutions to be simple and final. Complex systems don't work that way, and when it comes to working with nature, it is up to us to discover the best ways to create the outcomes we desire.

In my work, I oversee both a cattle ranch and a learning la'
focused on regenerative agriculture, a training and events center, a.
for supporting and advocating for sustainable food in our community. My
days are spent working with cowboys on how cattle-grazing can sequester
atmospheric carbon and protect wildlife habitat, developing educational programs on conservation and ranching, consulting with biologists on the newest
research, marketing grass-fed beef, and coordinating projects with our staff
and partners.

The TomKat Ranch Educational Foundation's mission—to produce
healthy food on working lands in a way that sustains the planet and inspires
others to action—provides a unifying vision for our work, yet requires a
wide array of human resources to put into practice. Coordinating such diversity among people can be a challenge, as cowboys and scientists don't always
agree on basic things like meeting etiquette or modern gender roles; but the
consensus-building process is one of the most important elements of our success, as that is where most of our breakthrough ideas come from—and where
they will need to come from in the changing times ahead.

The future of food will be collaboration, not specialization. Managers and
entrepreneurs who are able to bring to bear all of the best qualities of a complex team will be the most successful and valuable in creating sustainable operations. At TomKat, we have put a lot of thought and intention into building an
organization that can thrive because of, not in spite of, its diversity. At the core
of this effort are two important principles: shared values and clear expectations
for communication and collaboration.

I've learned that in agriculture, as in all fields, conflict is an inevitable part
of any team dynamic. While this can be frustrating at times, it is important to
remember as you start on your career that there is a critical difference between
discussing outcomes and arguing over intentions. We seek to focus our collective energy on goals and solutions and have created a set of values to give both
our team and partners a solid and relatable foundation on which to build collaboration. No matter what a person's background or education, the ideas he
or she brings to the table should reflect these values. While shared values do
not solve all communications challenges, they are incredibly helpful in bringing together a diverse group of people to guide decision making around complicated topics. We call our shared values the "6 Hs":

Happy animals: caring for our animals in ways that allow them to live healthy, natural, stress-free lives; injury or disease is addressed through natural methods whenever possible.

Healthy wilderness: caring for our land in ways that improve nutrient, carbon, and water cycles, build soil, support biodiversity, and sustain nature.

Healthy food: producing the healthiest, best-tasting products we can and in a way that cares for the land.

Hundred years: taking a long-term perspective and striving toward economically and ecologically sustainable practices that take the future of a changing climate into account.

Head: promoting innovative, out-of-the-box thinking and sharing results with others.

Heart: supporting our community—schools, institutions, and people—and being open to their input and help in return.

Creating structures for clear communication and collaboration is also very important. Everyone has something worthwhile to contribute, whether it is an innovative solution or a simple question that forces us to describe the problem in a different way. Facilitating such conversations, in which everyone is willing to share and listen, can be tough, especially with diverse teams. We have an unofficial policy known as "collaborative planning, independent execution," to create clear expectations for collaboration and give the individuals responsible for implementation the freedom to implement. For example, we give our land and livestock team considerable autonomy to adapt the grazing strategy to daily and seasonal changes on the land and in the herd; in return, the team is expected to host a weekly open planning meeting and a monthly land evaluation walk, and to write its yearly grazing plan together with our grass-fed beef business, our conservation science partners, and other stakeholders.

While these two strategies are not perfect, they offer a valuable and flexible method for tapping into diverse talents and skills. So surround yourself with a wide variety of people, perspectives, and tools as a critical part of your education and success. Listen; gather wisdom, insights, and ideas; and remember to invest plenty of time and intention to cultivate effective collaboration. It will pay off.

3. Pick solutions, not sides. "Sustainable" isn't an easy term to define—and it probably shouldn't be. There are so many variables to consider when designing for sustainability that it is foolish to expect the end results to look alike in different settings. In a world where change is the only constant, however, any business, farm, or individual claiming to be sustainable needs, above all, to be adaptable. Adaptation is the key to evolutionary and biological success, and we need to apply that lesson to our operations as well as to ourselves.

Those of us who are called to work with nature must be wary of bringing with us the human tendency toward dogma. To create and work with systems that are resilient and beneficial for our land, animals, and communities, we must stay open to tools and ideas from all potential sources.

My desire to pursue a career in conservation ranching began during a college summer working as a wrangler on a ranch in Wyoming. From the cowboys, I learned a way of life connected to land and animals—one very different from the way that most of the world works. Although the ranch I work on today has different methods of animal handling and land management, the lessons the cowboys taught me about respect for nature's powerful and unpredictable currents have connected me to life and land in a way that is both grand and humbling.

I've kept this perspective close to my heart because it can be easy at times to condemn those who are different from us, yet I have learned many times over that most landowners and managers share a common goal: to keep land, animals, people, and organizations healthy. Especially in the agricultural sector, we need to blend the best tools, perspectives, and ideas that everyone has to offer. Conventional agriculture can learn from sustainable agriculture's holistic perspective and total accounting of operational costs and benefits; sustainable agriculture can learn from conventional agriculture's scale and focus on efficiency. Ensuring that we're open to hearing the best advice requires releasing a hold on the labels we place on our neighbors and opening the lines of communication.

It's important to speak the language of those whom we want to convince or from whom we want to learn. At TomKat, we have developed a suite of communications tools for discussing what we do. We focus on rigorous science when speaking to policy makers and conservationists, on economics when speaking to ranchers and entrepreneurs, on nutrition and animal welfare when speaking to food advocates—and on all of the above when speaking to customers. This process of learning to communicate with different audiences has not only made us better at collaborating with a diversity of partners, it also teaches us new things and makes us stronger as a community of thinkers, practitioners, researchers, and consumers.

It's also important to take time to look at our decisions and management practices through multiple lenses and from multiple perspectives. Doing this gives us insight into opportunities and challenges we may have missed otherwise and exposes us to solutions we might not have known about before. For example, TomKat started its science program in order to help document and communicate the lessons of sustainable livestock production to policy makers and academics. Along the way and as a result of this work, we have become better land and animal managers through more rigorous record keeping and evaluation.

* * *

I hope these thoughts will be useful to you as you embark on this exciting journey. As a species, we are at an evolutionary crossroads where, for the first time in our history, we are the dominant ecological force on the planet. As a species still in its relative infancy, this is an incredible amount of power that we must learn to wield responsibly, and in quite a hurry. While this task may seem daunting, I hope the adventure will be rewarding. The future of sustainable food represents an unprecedented opportunity for innovative, skilled, observant, and diligent people to rise quickly past traditional barriers and make a true and lasting contribution to the health of our species and the planet we call home.

Wendy Millet is director of the TomKat Ranch Educational Foundation, a cattle ranch with a mission to raise healthy food on working lands in a way that sustains the planet and inspires others to action. She has worked on ranches in Wyoming and Montana and has spent more than twenty years in conservation, including twelve years at The Nature Conservancy. She serves on the boards of the Western Landowners Alliance and the California Council of Land Trusts and is cofounder of Gallop Ventures LLC, offering equine-guided leadership programs.

MARY-HOWELL MARTENS

Once, not very long ago, I was an innocent suburban Long Island teenager working at a children's community vegetable garden, gleefully shocking my family by declaring that I wanted to be a farmer. No one, absolutely no one, had been a farmer in my family for generations. This was the 1970s; the foodie movement had not yet begun. Farming held none of the allure it does today. Indeed, growing up in Long Island's heavily populated Nassau County, I didn't even know any farmers.

But there was something about that miracle of planting the seed, tending the plant, and then harvesting and eating. It was so basic, so integral to my core. It gave my time structure and purpose that I had never felt before. With my grades, I could have aimed for medical school or a PhD in biology—that was certainly what everyone was expecting—but I felt none of the enthusiasm or vocational calling that I felt for picking beans or my own ripe tomato or finding the buried gold of potatoes. Growing food: that was what mattered intensely, and on an entirely different plane from any other career I seriously considered.

Now, forty years later, having been a legitimate farmer for more than half that time, I still feel that thrill and sense of purpose and accomplishment, but with fewer illusions, a bit less innocence, and a whole lot more realism.

1. Farming is a great lifestyle, but it is seriously hard work. The hours are long, the risks are high, the uncontrollable forces are many, and the profit is unpredictable. I doubt there is any other career that demands that a person be proficient in so many diverse skills: a biologist, a mechanic, an accountant, an engineer, a physician, a meteorologist, a computer scientist, and a human resources specialist. But mostly you're a sweaty, dusty, blue-collar laborer, pulling long, unglamorous hours in the enervating July heat, the muddy April rain, the chilly January snow, the glorious first warm spring mornings of May, and the bright blue afternoons of October. You will lie awake worrying about the rain, the drought; wondering if the wind is damaging the buildings, whether the thunderstorm has turned to hail, whether you closed the gate or the cows got out, whether you forgot to turn off the tractor. You will be the first to see a newborn calf, an emerging seedling, the first rays of sunrise. You will smell rich, tilled earth, composted manure, rotten tomatoes, and diesel fuel. You will collapse from exhaustion at midnight, only to begin again at the break of dawn. The typical eight-hour American workday will cease to make any sense to you, for the work will never be done. At its very core, farming is not a job: it is a lifestyle that defines everything.

I recall one romantic Thanksgiving back when my husband, Klaas, and I were first married. We took a break briefly for the family dinner, but the rest of the day I handed wrenches and repair parts to Klaas, who was somewhere under our aging combine, and retrieved dropped bolts and tools from the icy water in the furrows. By that evening, the combine was going again and we harvested the field, the big machine swaying and roaring like a huge ship, gliding across the sea of darkened corn, the dust, corn husks, and snow flurries blowing past in the powerful headlights. As we watched the corn surge out of the auger into the wagon, we truly felt thanksgiving for this golden abundance.

As long as you go into farming expecting and preparing for this with eyes wide open, the rewards will be immense.

2. The grand choreography of work during the growing season is complex and stressful, especially if the weather doesn't cooperate for the desired timing of operations. Accept the fact from the very start that the ideal will rarely be achieved.

An effective farm manager must be able to see both the details and the whole picture at all times, agilely making well-reasoned and appropriate adjustments in operations and timing while staying calm under stress and frustration. You must take a balanced whole-farm view, day to day and season to season, with a positive attitude and vision.

No farm manager is perfect; absolutely everyone falls short. All jobs can be done by one extraordinary and exhaustingly overworked person or shared among all the available people according to ability, interest, and need. All the jobs on a farm are important. As Klaas regularly says, the most important job on a farm is the one that is *not* getting done.

3. Diversity is the greatest source of risk management on a farm. Diverse crop rotation is our best defense against insects, diseases, and weeds and the best way to manage soil health, soil fertility, and organic matter. It is also our best defense against weather extremes, equipment breakdowns, lack of available labor, and market fluctuations. With a diverse crop rotation on a grain farm, we can be both planting and harvesting every week, from June to November, spreading out our labor and equipment demands to a fairly manageable level.

But there is a downside to crop diversity. When you have too many crops all competing for attention and resources, it can be difficult to do the right thing for all "the kids." Increasing crop diversity can open up new, engaging markets, especially into profitable food-grade products, but learning how to meet the quality and logistical specifications for each new market can be extremely daunting and can rob other existing crops and activities of sufficient time and attention.

Consciously balance the benefits of additional diversity with a strong, cold dose of reality. Carefully evaluate each new opportunity in advance to predict how it will fit into the existing operation. Not everything is worth it, even profitable and successful opportunities, if they jeopardize your ability to keep up with existing demands.

4. Farming can be all-consuming, especially at certain times of the year, and without a plan to protect an acceptable level of personal balance, you may find the farm takes all. Farming will invariably define your family, your self-esteem, your financial choices, your self-image, your priorities, and your time. It will profoundly shape how you interpret life and death, weather, money, time, food, community, exercise, and faith. Make sure your spouse or partner and family are fully on board, and be willing to honestly evaluate whether everyone is defining balance in the same way. Accept that if you are the farmer and your spouse or partner is not, that does not make you intrinsically "righter" than they are.

I remember one Wednesday in November when our youngest son, Daniel, was in kindergarten. For a birthday treat, we invited his entire school class out to the farm for tractor rides, fun with the animals, and a campfire lunch beside the pond. Those kids had such a great time riding around in the big tractors with Klaas, throwing stale bread to the pigs, and roasting marshmallows over the fire. A few weeks later, I laughed when one of the other mothers said her son came home from the party filled with envy that "Daniel's parents stay home and play with him all day long." His friends did not see the endless hours and hard work. Instead, they legitimately saw that both of Daniel's parents were fully there and engaged with their son on a weekday afternoon.

Learn to recognize and appreciate the special kind of balance that is unique to the self-employed.

5. Farming can be a lonely job that is hard on relationships. Communion with soil, animals, and plants is invigorating, inspiring, and spiritually uplifting. The freedom to be without a boss, a time clock, and office politics is true independence. Walking out into the fresh morning air, with the whole day ahead to plan and accomplish, gives you a terrific sense of maturity and opportunity.

But spending the entire day alone on a tractor or in the field can be tedious, boring, isolated, and downright lonely. Some people are well suited to working alone, while many people are not; they rapidly miss the camaraderie, distraction, and pace-setting of coworkers, and their productivity plummets. It is best to evaluate this about yourself now, before you choose a farm environment that doesn't suit you.

At many times of the year, your leisure hours will not match those of your nonfarming friends, making social life challenging. Your friends may not understand why you can't go away for a weekend vacation. Developing a functional social life, off-farm activities, and even the occasional vacation is important to maintain a healthy perspective and enthusiasm, and while this can be complicated, it is not impossible.

Working long, hard, tiring hours with your spouse or partner can stress any relationship, often to the breaking point. Unlike the romanticized image of Laura Ingalls Wilder farm life, farming today is actually quite hard on marriages. The strain of work; cooperation; fatigue; financial and seasonal stress; differing expectations; traditional gender roles; and the equitable sharing of responsibilities for childcare, house, and barn can be seriously challenging for many couples, in complex and insidious ways that the typical urban two-career couple will never understand. If you are lucky, a farm can actually strengthen a couple and a family as all work together toward a common goal, but all too often the farm becomes "wife number one," demanding an inordinate share of time, resources, money, emotion, and attention. Both partners need to clearly recognize this as quite a reasonable possibility. Both need to understand the stress and pain it will cause and then consciously, constantly, and proactively work to minimize it.

6. When you are a farmer, you will never stop learning. Farming requires you to constantly learn new things, sharpen your observations, adjust your conclusions, question your assumptions, go back and read some more, and then make changes. It's a career in which the variables change each year, as you constantly adapt to climate change, consumer whims, and new technology. It keeps you on the risky but heady edge of success and failure for months on end.

For the right person, farming can be the dream job that will draw on absolutely every skill and ability you have, develop ones you never knew you could, and provide constant learning opportunities.

After we had been farming organically for a few years, we started thinking about writing the definitive book about organic grain production. But we were busy raising a family and farming, so the book went on the back burner, only for it to become apparent that we might never be able to write that definitive book: our understanding, our knowledge, and even our degree of success and the effectiveness of our choices changed each year. Now we know that we never will "have it down," that each year will present new challenges. But, through the process, we have learned that while we may complain mightily about the stress, we also thrive on the adrenaline and unpredictability of farming.

Being born into a farming family may provide advantages of land and experience, but it guarantees neither that a young person truly wants to farm nor that he or she is well suited to the lifestyle. A young person without a farming background but with sufficient motivation can acquire the skills, and he or she will often come into farming with a more open mind, a more diverse background, and without the baggage of "we've always done it that way" that can hamper innovation.

7. Farming requires handling money in a completely different way. If you are currently working a job with a weekly paycheck that compensates you for every hour you have worked, your income is predictable and reliable. If you farm, all of that will become history.

As a farmer, you will probably no longer be compensated "fairly" for the hours you work. You will work more hours each week, and if you average your farm gross income over the hours of everyone working, your hourly value is likely to be significantly below minimum wage. If you have employees, they may even end up making more than you do.

As a farmer, you must also become accustomed to the fact that money will not come at regular intervals. Instead money will come in as "slugs" at harvest, generally months after the expenses pile up. Self-discipline and budgeting become very important, for whatever you make this year at harvest must pay a full year's worth of family and farm expenses, plus the cost of putting in next year's crop. Winter may be a lean time, so prepare for that.

You will start thinking about expenses differently. If you live on the farm, perhaps your vehicle is a farm truck and you raise much of your own food. If you work especially hard and have a bumper crop with good markets, your income can swell, but it can also plummet unexpectedly with crop failures and falling prices.

Money management on most farms requires careful planning, budgeting, self-discipline, maturity, and wishful thinking. When money arrives at harvest, it can never be viewed as "profit," for there are twelve months of expenses that must eat off that money. Farms with a year-round enterprise like dairy, eggs, or greenhouse crops may find money management easier, although their expenses are higher and the possibility for vacation during the winter becomes remote.

* * *

By now, are you wondering: Had I known this before I married a farmer, would I have chosen this path?

I was young and idealistic, with far more knowledge than experience, as much in love with the idea of being a farmer as I was with the farmer himself.

Perhaps that innocent, youthful enthusiasm is necessary to send us into such new, risky territory. If we knew all the hazards, who would go? We firmly believed we would succeed; we never considered the possibility that we would not, and so we went boldly forward, ready to work hard, have fun, meet interesting people, and grow good food.

We didn't expect it to be easy, but we did expect to succeed. I wish the same for you.

Mary-Howell Martens manages Lakeview Organic Grain, an organic feed and seed business in upstate New York, shipping organic dairy and small-animal feed throughout the Northeast. She also assists her husband, Klaas, and son Peter as they farm sixteen hundred acres of certified-organic grain crops.

RICK BAYLESS

I have a friend in Ireland who runs a much-lauded cooking school, one that turns out well-trained chefs who know more than simply how to measure and sauté or bake. I know that because the first lesson she teaches isn't even in the kitchen, but in a corner of the vast gardens that surround it. That's where she shares the first recipe—the one for compost.

It's a shame that we live in a world that exalts specialists over generalists. Sure, the world is a complex place—more and more complex the more we understand it—and it takes a lifetime to master one small parcel of it. But I've come to appreciate how much more effective I am in my life, whether I'm creating something delicious at the stove or I'm at a computer writing about it, when I understand how everything is connected: how the ingredients I am working with are the expression of a particular stretch of earth at a particular moment in time; how the way we transform those ingredients in the kitchen reflects a treasure trove of details about our history, our aesthetics, even our physiology.

I know it's popular these days for chefs to say that they want to do as little to their direct-from-the-farm ingredients as possible. In spirit, I understand what they're trying to say: they're offering a well-deserved tribute to the skillful farmers who've too long gone nameless and underappreciated. But, honestly, that's not what's going on in most of their kitchens. We are human beings, and since time immemorial, we've been consumed with the alchemy of the kitchen. We memorialize cooks who transform beautiful ingredients into beautiful preparations that lead us to new ways of understanding and appreciating and enjoying.

And what's often left out of that progression is the logical extension to the table. Those beautifully crafted ingredients in that beautifully crafted dish work their magic on a cluster of people at a table, becoming the catalyst—if we're paying attention—to creating community in unique and enduring ways.

At my restaurants in Chicago, I've been building relationships with farmers for nearly three decades, long before the string of words "farm to table" had been formed by anyone's mouth. I felt the need to forge those relationships from the earliest years because of a lesson I'd learned while living in Mexico, before my wife and I decided to settle in Chicago. Every region in Mexico that was famous for its cooking was also famous for the produce that was grown there. Where there was great agriculture, it became clear to me, great cuisine followed. The fields around Toluca provide lush greens that are celebrated in everything from market tacos to elegant braises. The chili fields that blanket the state of Oaxaca provide the essentials for that state's famous array of *moles*. The beans and corn so abundant in Mexico's Bajío provide the nuts and bolts of a cuisine that has created variety and brilliance from such humble ingredients.

I wanted to make great food in my restaurants, so I knew that I had to discover and build upon what the local farmers were crafting. The problem was, there were almost none of them back in the eighties—not even a single farmers' market in the city of Chicago.

The essential flow from earth to produce to kitchen to table wasn't transparent when we opened our restaurants, and I knew that lack of transparency would hinder the realization of my dreams. I knew that the hands that tilled the earth and harvested the produce needed to be the hands of folks I considered partners in my bigger mission. I knew the hands holding knives and forks at the table needed to be partners too; folks who understood—or were willing to learn—why the food tasted as good as it did. To create great cuisine, farmers couldn't be simply suppliers and restaurant guests couldn't be considered consumers. We had to march along arm in arm.

Now as I reflect on how far we've gone down this odd little path we've chosen—we offer dishes that are deeply rooted in the regional cuisines of Mexico, crafted almost exclusively with locally grown ingredients—one thing is clear to me: the farmers I rely on the most have turned out to be the ones who love to cook and eat. Not only are most of them ardent cooks but also they're always enthusiastic to understand how we've transformed their produce or meat or grains. And it seems that our best restaurant cooks and servers are the ones who share vegetables or herbs from their own gardens or the ones who can't wait to spend a day on one of our partner farms. And our most regular guests—the ones we call the Frontera family—are the ones who are always stepping into the kitchen for cooking tips or to grab a handful of some hard-to-find herb to weave into a dish at home.

Yes, any one of these people could say "I'm a farmer" or "I'm a cook" or "I'm a restaurant guest." But the truth is, we're part of a single community.

Rick Bayless is the award-winning chef and co-owner of restaurants in Chicago, including Frontera Grill, Topolobampo, and Xoco. He has authored nine best-selling cookbooks and hosted PBS's *Mexico: One Plate at a Time* for more than a decade. Besides winning the James Beard Foundation's highest honors, he is the recipient of Mexico's Order of the Aztec Eagle, the highest award given to nonnatives who have done great work for the country.

DANIELLE NIERENBERG

I didn't grow up as a farmer, but I grew up in a farming community. I was born in Defiance, Missouri, a small town with a big name about forty-five minutes west of St. Louis.

My parents were the kind of city people who wanted to raise their kids in the fresh air. I had a pretty idyllic childhood. We had a huge garden, my mom canned everything that would fit into a jar, I raised rabbits and ducks, and I had a pony, which still makes all of my friends jealous.

I grew up around farm kids. We played on their dads' tractors and combines—I know, not the safest farm activity. We ran through cornfields, and cow tipping was a real thing.

But I wanted nothing to do with any of it. Farming, to me, was boring; to be honest, I thought it was dumb. I didn't get it. When I looked at the rows and rows of corn and soybeans, all I felt was trapped. As I grew up and became an environmentalist, I even blamed farmers for destroying forests and biodiversity.

So I hightailed it out of there, vowing never to look back and certainly never to be involved in farming. I was going to save the world, and like so many other idealistic twenty-two-year-olds, I joined the Peace Corps. I was sent to the Dominican Republic. There, as luck would have it, I ended up meeting a lot of farmers. They changed my whole life.

In the Dominican Republic, for the first time I saw the connections between how we produce and how we consume food, and their negative and positive impacts on public health and the environment. I rode around on the backs of motorcycles with extension agents, who introduced me to farmers who were growing traditional crops or shade-grown coffee or raising bees, and I finally got it—how important farming communities were and are to food and nutrition security and environmental protection. It wasn't an epiphany, but a slow realization that I was the dumb one—not the farmers.

I'm so grateful to those Dominican farmers. They led me to get an MS at Tufts University's Friedman School of Nutrition Science and Policy. They led me to seek internships about international agriculture. And they led me to my current position as the president of Food Tank. The best part of my job is getting to interview farmers from all over the world and learn about the innovations they're developing to combat climate change, preserve biodiversity, enrich soils, and produce more nutritious foods. At this point, I've visited sixty-plus countries in Sub-Saharan Africa, Asia, and Latin America and have spent countless days in fields and on farms scribbling notes as farmers talk about their challenges in producing food. My biggest honor in life is sharing their stories.

I now know that there is no more important job than being involved in the food system and that small farmers produce at least 70 percent of the world's food. Your efforts, along with those of five hundred million other family farmers, are changing the way the world eats. We now understand that farmers are more than just farmers: you're businesswomen and -men, entrepreneurs and innovators, caretakers of rich cultural traditions, and stewards of the land who deserve to be recognized for the ecosystem services you provide that benefit us all.

As you begin your career in farming, please know that there will be people who will dismiss what you're doing and think it's not important. But know that eventually those dumb kids will grow up and appreciate your efforts to nourish both people and the planet.

Danielle Nierenberg is president of Food Tank and an expert on sustainable agriculture and food issues. She founded Food Tank in 2013 as a nonprofit organization focused on building a global community for safe, healthy, nourished eaters.

ALLAN SAVORY

Dear Chris,

Your grandparents* asked me to write to you. They say I helped save their struggling farm and family fifty years ago, and they asked if I would please help you, starting to farm as you are. I am only too pleased to help, although I will have to compress sixty years' learning into this letter to at least get you started on the right foot. While I can help you succeed, it won't help you and your family if other farmers do not also succeed. For this reason, I will refer to your millennial generation, who are, in my view, the most important ever because American agriculture is at a turning point. People do not see it as a turning point, but history will, I assure you.

I will explain things on a larger scale, so you fully understand the situation facing your generation, and then understand what you can do on your own farm. What I pass on is not, I assure you, from any brilliance of my own, but from a long life struggling to first understand and then find simple, practical solutions to the seemingly impossible problems associated with agriculture. These problems do not arise from crop production alone but from all production of food and fiber from the world's land and waters. Running fisheries, forestry, keeping livestock, hunting wildlife: all are agriculture. We grow crops on about 20 percent of both America's and the world's land area. I mention this because I hear you love growing things, but you are going to have to pay attention to livestock as well.

The big picture is depressing, but your generation will need to grasp it to truly understand the need for rapid and dramatic changes; otherwise, you will fall into accepting small, incremental change that is simply not going to work. So let's briefly look at the current reality.

---

*A family in the Karoo desert of South Africa whom Savory helped in the 1970s with a different approach to management.

Overall, American agriculture is a disaster, producing the least-nutritious food with the most environmental damage ever known. And through education, policy, USAID, and other means, the United States is promoting such agriculture globally. Every year, we produce ten tons of dead, eroding soil per human alive. And here in America, we have a crisis of obesity and other food-related illnesses, resulting annually in more deaths than were suffered in any year of the two world wars. Hardly a week goes by without the publication of yet more studies showing hundreds of billions of dollars of environmental damage from nitrogen pollution, the loss of bees, the connection of pesticides and herbicides to cancer, and the loss of soil life. Recently, the Union of Concerned Scientists reported that today's industrial chemical agriculture is inarguably unsustainable. Such information is finally becoming public despite a multibillion-dollar propaganda campaign promoting the corporate myth that only industrial chemical agriculture can feed the world's growing population.

This situation is compounded by climate change. I was shocked recently to read a report by an international team of scientists, mathematicians, and philosophers at Oxford's Future of Humanity Institute. They laid out the five greatest threats to human survival. Climate change was not among them because, as they explained, some regions of our planet would still be habitable!

Because agriculture's role in climate change is trivialized, let me describe the basics. Climate change is believed to result from four atmospheric pollutants: carbon dioxide, methane, nitrous oxide, and black carbon. Unfortunately, soil degradation and desertification also contribute to climate change. Of these four pollutants, roughly half are by-products of fossil fuel combustion. The other half come from agriculture—from the burning of grasslands and forests and the destruction of soil, mainly. Therefore, even after we stop using fossil fuels, climate change will persist because of agriculture.

To halt the pollutants from agriculture and reverse desertification cannot be done with any technology even imaginable in science fiction because, put simply, the agricultural problem is an ecological or biological problem. To remove the now-excessive amount of carbon in the atmosphere and safely store it for thousands of years cannot be done in the already-acidifying oceans. It cannot be done by planting trees, shrubs, or grasses because they are part of the normal ambient carbon cycle of life, which, in essence, means carbon is absorbed by the vegetation but only stored temporarily, until the plants die. The place we can safely store carbon for thousands of years without unintended consequences is in the world's soils—mainly grassland soils.

If you wonder why I say grassland soils, just ask yourself why the world's great grain-growing regions are found on the deep, carbon-rich soils of ancient grasslands. Grassland soils developed over millions of years with an amazing synergy with the vast numbers of grazing animals kept bunched together and moving by predators. When grasses are grazed, they draw energy for their regrowth from roots, leaving dead root organic matter in the soil. As leaves regrow, so too do roots, and the constant pattern of graze and root recovery literally pumps carbon deep into the ground, forming the carbon-rich soils that industrial agriculture is destroying. Tree roots do not pulse like this when their leaves drop, and so do not pump anywhere near as much carbon deep into the ground.

Most people now live in cities detached from ecological reality—not understanding that without agriculture, America would not have orchestras, museums, universities, corporations, the military, government, towns, or cities. It is not rocket science to understand that the only wealth that can sustain any nation ultimately is derived from the photosynthetic process—from plants growing on regenerating soils. I read Alan Greenspan's autobiography to see how well the former head of the US Federal Reserve understood agriculture as the foundation of the American economy; I found only one passing reference to agriculture! We face a crisis of massive ecological illiteracy. Little do those people know who warn of the suffering that poor rural communities will encounter from climate change: it is our cities that will face the greatest suffering, violence, and death unless urban people wake up soon.

Now perhaps you understand why your generation needs new thinking, open minds, and collaboration throughout agriculture at a level never before seen. Organic, permaculture, sustainable, and industrial: all are in the same boat together in a stormy sea, but every American citizen is in the boat with you, although not knowing the boat even exists or that the perfect storm is approaching.

But enough of doomsday stuff, because new thinking is emerging, and I am excited about what your generation can now do.

Chris, I know you intend to farm organically. That is good, because agriculture obviously needs to be based on what I will call the biological sciences. Industrial agriculture, as we know, is not; it is based on chemistry, smart marketing of technology, large-scale monocultures, and low-nutrition fast food. (Long ago, I said publicly that Americans should fear the USDA more than the USSR.) So you are on the right path, although you biological farmers represent only 1 percent of American agriculture.

I urge you not to fall into the trap of saying that all we need to do is increase the amount of organically grown crops and grass-fed cattle. Where civilizations failed to endure, the problem can be traced to environmental damage—and those past civilizations did not have the fossil fuels, machinery, and chemicals that we have today. All crops were organic, all livestock fed grass. Heed history and understand that what is needed is a truly new *regenerative* agriculture—a term that I first heard from Bob Rodale, organic farmer and publisher, when he recognized that agriculture had to regenerate society, economies, and soils.

Your generation simply has to develop this new, regenerative agriculture. And while it may seem daunting, I am going to paraphrase Winston Churchill speaking at another profoundly dangerous time: if something has to be done and all your experts say it cannot be done, then change your experts and do it.

The problem is essentially one of dealing with enormous social, economic, and environmental complexity, and there are no experts. Experts in the current ways are as useful as expert candlemakers were to developing electric lights. Your generation may feel daunted by your lack of farming experience, but you also enjoy a tremendous advantage over those who know so much about organic and present agriculture. I have worked with thousands of people, from illiterate villagers to PhDs, and have never seen ignorance block learning. The only things that block learning—and I'm no exception—are what we already know and our pride, or ego, associated with that.

Clearly your generation is taking over as the most important ever in history, and you have the task of redefining agriculture entirely, if tragedy beyond imagination is to be avoided. Thankfully, you have two great advantages. First, you lack experience and thus are not hampered by the greatest vested interest in the world—the expert egos. Second, surveys show more young people today than ever before want to live truly meaningful lives.

Developing the new agriculture is almost certainly going to provide ample opportunity for your generation to live meaningful lives. I am excited for you, and for millions of other young families as they come to understand how much they are needed on the land and how richly rewarding farm life can once again be.

At my age, I am in the departure lounge and will not be sharing the exciting future of agriculture with you. All I can do is pass on what I've learned over the past sixty years, since I became truly alarmed at what I saw. I pass on what saved your grandparents and is now being practiced by thousands of farmers, ranchers, pastoralists, and collaborating scientists over millions of acres on six continents affiliated through the Savory Institute network of locally led and managed hubs. What began as a new way of regenerating manmade deserts using livestock became today's Savory method of Holistic Management, in which we use a holistic framework to bring all of the complexity of society, economy, and environment together to bear on any aspect of agriculture. Where Holistic Management is practiced, it is proving consistently successful in regenerating soil life, and it is replicable, so we seem to be on the right path.

The theory behind Holistic Management was provided by the South African statesman and philosopher Jan Smuts in 1926 when he wrote *Holism and Evolution*. Albert Einstein, by the way, said he believed two constructs would play an important role in mankind's future: his theory of relativity and Smuts's holism.

Although Holistic Management was developed by me, nothing comes from one mind only. Over decades of learning how to deal with first desertification and then agriculture's complexity, I stood on the shoulders of past giants: ecologists and thinkers such as Smuts, Aldo Leopold, Sir Albert Howard, André Voisin, and others. Along my path, thousands of caring and concerned people helped me: farmers, ranchers, pastoralists, wildlife biologists, foresters, and individuals from universities and government agencies.

By the early 1980s we had the holistic framework in place and thousands of people were being trained and spreading the practice widely. Farsighted USDA officials asked me to train some two thousand USDA staff, land grant university faculty members, and World Bank and USAID officials. Those people analyzed hundreds of government policies dealing with the usual problems—among them drought, flood, invasive plants, desertification of western rangelands, failing small towns, and endangered species—and they concluded that all of their current policies and projects were likely to fail and to lead to unintended consequences. Because faulty policies are so damaging, I urged all participants to look critically at the holistic framework, including the idea of reversing desertification using the Savory methods of Holistic Planned

Grazing, and to find any flaws in either the logic or the science. They found none, so again, we seem to be on the right path.

Let me give you a brief account of what led us to develop the holistic framework, because this highlights two profoundly simple causes of both historical and present agricultural problems: the vilification of livestock for causing desertification and climate change, and the fact that management has always been mechanistic in a holistic world. Years ago, I realized that with so much going wrong over centuries, yet with so many brilliant minds among us that we can explore space, it had to be a systemic issue rather than any lack of knowledge on our farms or among our experts. And so it is.

Farmers throughout the ages and, in fact, all humans have a profoundly simple, genetically embedded way of doing things: we are tool-using animals. Unless you go to the nearest river, you cannot even drink water without a cup, mug, or tap. We believe we have thousands of tools to manage our environment. So we do, but these essential tools fall into just three categories: we have technology in all its many forms, from the days of sticks and stones to the present marvels; we have fire; and we have the concept of actively resting the environment to allow recovery from damage or from lost species. That is it; no more tools ever. We cannot even use water to irrigate except by using technology, just as we use a cup to drink water. It was our ever-improving technology that enabled past farmers to plant crops and redirect water, and it is easy to understand how we were lured into industrial agriculture.

But there is no tool that could have prevented or can reverse the world's and America's serious desertification. Environments that alternate seasonally between humid and dry dominate the world's land area, and grasses provide the main soil cover in such regions—more so in places where rainfall is less. These grasslands are where the soil life, plants, and large grazing animals and predators all coevolved together. Ever since mankind killed off most wild ungulates and predators and replaced them with a few domesticated animals, deserts have been expanding.

Soil life cannot be regenerated using the three tools I mention above. No technology even imaginable in science fiction can replace the role of billions of large grazing animals over most of the world's land. Fire cannot. Resting land does not except in regions of perennial humidity. This is why I said in a recent TED talk on desertification that we have no option but to open our minds to the unthinkable and use much-vilified livestock, managed holistically, to mimic nature's past work in creating the grasslands and their rich soil. Thousands of people are now doing this. Like all counterintuitive scientific insights in history, this concept has had to endure fifty years of ridicule and opposition, but that is finally dying down as this commonsense idea spreads.

On the ranch in Zimbabwe where I live much of the year, we are now regenerating soils and river flow, increasing wildlife, and showing we can produce five times the local crop yields without machinery, fossil fuels, or chemical fertilizer—all by using livestock as the main tool. We began Holistic Management on the ranch when it was in very poor condition, running a hundred head of cattle and later ramping up to five hundred head. After eight average-to-poor rain years, we are now increasing the cattle herd to one thousand to keep pace with the land's productivity: soil cover and soil life are returning, and all plants are now growing better while wildlife returns. The contrast with the still-deteriorating nearby national parks is greater every year.

I know this sounds too good to be true, and some call me a snake-oil salesman, but many conservation experts are coming to realize the benefits of Holistic Management. As Dr. M. Sanjayan, at the time a senior scientist with The Nature Conservancy, said about this work on his PBS series, *Earth: A New Wild*: "[Savory's] message is an extraordinarily powerful one, and it could be the best thing, the absolute best thing that conservation has ever discovered. In a million years, I never thought that cows could be so beneficial for the wildlife I love.... As an ecologist I was taught that people, and especially their livestock, are the enemy of wildlife; but my journey from Africa to the Arctic to here in Montana is forcing me to rethink everything I know about conservation."

By adding the tool of livestock to our small toolbox, we can now regenerate agriculturally damaged soils everywhere—especially where resting the land leads to serious desertification and where annual rainfall is between one and twenty inches. Adding this tool, however, did not address the failure of past organic farmers to preserve the soil their civilizations depended upon in regions of high rainfall and perennial humidity. Nor did it explain the erratic results I was achieving in my early work with ranchers. All we had learned was to add a tool in seasonally dry grasslands—a tool not necessarily needed in perennially humid environments where there never were vast numbers of grazing animals, because most herbivores were insects. In such environments, resting the land is the most powerful tool we have to restore life. Something was still missing.

Once more, the solution proved to be profoundly simple. We always have objectives, be it to grow corn, kill invasive weeds, build a dam, buy toothpaste, or get an education. Government policies, too, have objectives. Common sense will tell you that objectives always need a reason or context, and our management objectives do always have a context. The context is always something like "meeting a need or desire," "making a profit," "increasing production," "providing employment," or "a problem being experienced."

Any management objective or action that has no context, or has too simple a context, is a loose cannon, likely to result in unintended consequences—imagine lighting a fire with no reason or context. When managing both organizations and agriculture, it is simply not possible to avoid social, environmental, and economic complexity. Everything we manage is complex by definition. Reducing the context for management actions to achieve a specific objective, goal, or mission to such simple contexts as need, desire, profit, or problem is reductionist management, be it a decision you make for your farm or a government policy. Yet even today, sophisticated teams of integrated experts, fully conscious that a policy will have social and environmental consequences, develop policy objectives with the context reduced to the specific problem being addressed, be it noxious weeds, drugs, or terrorism. We have managed similarly for thousands of years, with the context behind our actions too simple, too reductive, for our cultures' social, environmental, and economic complexity. *Here lies the profoundly simple systemic reason for most tragedies we face and have ever faced.* So common are unintended consequences that we talk of the Law of Unintended Consequences as a humorous reminder that we should have more humility when dealing with the world around us.

Interestingly, the sociobiologist Rebecca Costa, in her book, *The Watchman's Rattle: Thinking Our Way Out of Extinction*, concluded that past civilizations failed not only because of their agriculture but also because their societies could not address the complexity of rising population and a deteriorating environment. Instead, they turned to faith and sacrifices, while shelving the problems for future generations. Sound familiar?

The hardest part of our task is to develop an overarching holistic context in management as the context for fulfilling needs and desires, achieving profit, or addressing problems; this is a new concept not previously found in any branch of science, philosophy, or religion. You are probably wondering what a holistic context looks like. This is the generalized holistic context I use when assessing any action on a farm or policy, imagining myself part of that community:

> We want stable families living peaceful lives in prosperity and physical security while free to pursue our own spiritual or religious beliefs. We want adequate, nutritious food and clean water, good education and health in balanced lives with time for family, friends, and community, and with leisure for cultural and other pursuits. All of this to be ensured, for many generations to come, on a foundation of regenerating soils and biologically diverse communities on Earth's land and in her rivers, lakes, and oceans.

Assessing actions through such a holistic context, rather than simply looking at a specific need, desire, or problem, produces different conclusions.

I think you will agree that most people want lives like that, tied to a life-supporting environment. But we argue, fight, and kill one another because we have different objectives without a holistic context. Provided that learning is not blocked by what we already know or by our egos, people can learn to make decisions addressing the complexity on any farm or in any policy or setting literally within days.

Earlier I mentioned how thousands of USDA and other officials successfully used the holistic framework to analyze their own policies. Still, there were some academics who simply could not stomach the idea of using livestock to reverse desertification, and so nothing changed. Since then, I have had thirty years to learn more about why things change so slowly in society. The reason is really because almost everything we do is controlled by our many organizations or institutions that reflect the prevailing beliefs of society. And when truly new counterintuitive information emerges, institutions simply do not change without a significant shift in society's views. Eric Ashby researched how new knowledge gets into society, examining Britain and America over the past two hundred years as his case study. He found that in democratic societies, new knowledge only becomes accepted through grassroots change. So do not look to or expect leadership from any university, company, or organization; it will come from ordinary people.

I mention this because you millennial farmers should not waste your energy on fighting, criticizing, or trying to change corporations, universities, the USDA, or the farming organizations that support industrial agriculture. You need to concentrate your efforts on shifting public opinion. Period.

Because the battlefield is public opinion and not corporate boardrooms, political parties, or Washington, DC, you need to know that the leaders shifting public opinion are independent authors, bloggers, artists, filmmakers, and keynote speakers. Work with them, because only a well-informed public will bring down the "Berlin Wall" that separates a pervasive agriculture based in chemistry and the marketing of technology from a regenerative agriculture based in the biological sciences. This wall has been held up by an unhealthy alliance of corporate agriculture using obscene sums of money to influence politicians, universities, research, laws, regulations, and farm policy.

You millennial generation farmers will have to demonstrate the ability to produce more nutritious food per acre while regenerating soil. You will have to provide truthful and convincing evidence and get the information out to American families. *Fast Food Nation*, both the book by Eric Schlosser and later the film by Richard Linklater, as well as writers and speakers like Robb Wolf, are doing much to alert the public to the full social, health, environmental, and economic costs of industrial agriculture. Writers such as Wendell Berry, Sir Albert Howard, André Voisin, and others have laid both the scientific and philosophical groundwork. Swelling the flood is a new generation of authors such as Judy Schwartz, Nicolette Hahn Niman, and John Fullerton and speakers such as Gabe Brown, Colin Seis, and Jason Rowntree, to name but a few who are highlighting the scientific understanding of the unbroken chain from abundant soil life to healthy people and economy.

Let's now look at what you personally can do today, tomorrow, and for the rest of your meaningful life. When faced with situations like yours, I stop and ask myself, what would I do?

First, I would build a solid business foundation for my family. To make my farm truly profitable—one that regenerates soil, remember—I would use the Holistic Management framework and its holistic financial planning process, developed for agriculture, based on the only true sustainable wealth. In the 1980s Deb Stinner and colleagues at Ohio State University studied early adopters across America, and they averaged 300 percent more profit. Over approximately the same time span, six hundred thousand American farmers went bankrupt, and suicide was the leading cause of farm deaths. You can learn immediately about holistic financial planning from textbook, handbook, and electronic self-learning materials available from the Savory Institute's website, savory.global.

Using Holistic Planned Grazing, I would integrate livestock with crop production to regenerate soil as the most efficient way to deal with the full complexity of your farming situation. Today's fads of rotational or mob grazing do give reasonable results in more humid regions, but on large ranches and public lands and particularly in lower-rainfall regions, they lead to desertification.

I would join the growing swell of regenerative farmers learning together and seek good mentors—farmers like Gabe Brown, Will Harris, Joel Salatin, and others who are demonstrating inarguably that by integrating livestock with crops, they are regenerating soils and producing more nutritious food per acre than industrial agriculture will ever be able to do.

I would attend workshops and conferences to meet soil scientists like Elaine Ingham and Christine Jones to learn about their research showing the mind-boggling complexity of soil life. At such places, you will meet the growing numbers of excellent writers and speakers connecting the dots from soil life to a healthy, prosperous nation.

I would collaborate with fellow farmers and others who are developing markets while educating city families through food. Above all, because political and economic power has shifted from rural communities to cities, I would not simply preach to the choir but get the regenerative agriculture message into cities. Here is where marketing through health-conscious restaurants, food stores, and gyms, as Robb Wolf so ably does, helps reach the majority of urban citizens.

Even if you 1 percent of organic farmers keep making the incredible progress you are making and increase your numbers to, say, 15 percent in twenty years, you will still not even be at the table when government makes policies—and without holistically sound policies, the game is over. Better-informed citizens insisting on one unifying idea will create an even playing field to turn that around. *The one idea that should permeate the public mind is that policy needs to be developed holistically*, because every sane American wants the same things, and agriculture as the basis of civilization has to be apolitical—an idea that no scientist or politician can oppose. To retain the present practice of siloed experts, subjected to lobbying pressure and corporate and political-party passions in a reductionist manner, will become unthinkable. If we move to holistic thinking, not only will all of agriculture become regenerative but also the US government will no longer push flawed policy and USAID on other nations, thus saving trillions of dollars and billions of lives.

Chris, I do hope what I have outlined here you will find helpful. My wife, Jody, joins me in sending our love, and we hope one day to meet your husband and enjoy wonderful, nutritious food at your table.

Sincerely,
Allan

A former wildlife biologist, farmer, and politician, Zimbabwean-born **Allan Savory** made a significant breakthrough in the 1960s in understanding what was causing the degradation and desertification of the world's grassland ecosystems and worked with farmers, eventually on four continents, to develop sustainable solutions. In 2009 he cofounded the Savory Institute in Boulder, Colorado, to promote large-scale restoration of the world's grasslands through Holistic Management. In 2003 he was awarded Australia's International Banksia Award for the "person doing the most for the environment on a global scale," and in 2010 he won the Buckminster Fuller Challenge for work that has "significant potential to solve humanity's most pressing problems."

MARION NESTLE

Congratulations on choosing a profession that is socially, philosophically, ethically, morally, and—one dearly wishes—economically satisfying. Few jobs in our society can lead to the pride, pleasure, and sheer fun that come from growing food for yourself, your friends and family, or for others, in ways that promote human health and protect the environment.

At issue, of course, is how to make a living from doing what you love. Other writers in this volume no doubt have plenty to say about how to acquire land, equipment, seeds, animals, and people to help you get started and bring your production to the point of sale. They will talk to you about the importance of conserving soil and water, treating workers fairly, and producing food under conditions that are healthiest for plants and animals.

But I want to talk about something else: the politics of what you are doing.

In choosing to farm sustainably, you are presenting an explicit critique—a slap in the face—of America's industrial agricultural system. By growing crops and raising animals without harmful chemicals and feedlots, you are a living reminder of the harm done to the land, animals, and people by industrial farming methods. Whether or not you see it that way, the very existence of your farm and your ways of farming make a political statement.

Along with everything else you are learning to do, you must also learn to engage with the political system. Politics is a team sport. It's not something you can do alone. You will want to look for opportunities to join other farmers in cooperatives, unions, clubs, trade associations, and any other forum devoted to unity as strength. You will want to work with community and national organizations to make your needs and views heard by your local and state governments. You will want to learn the names of your congressional representatives and senators, go and meet their staff, and use your knowledge and skills to call and write them whenever you think they should be doing something to help you or to stop some rule or regulation that will make your life more difficult.

As part of a long-term strategy for promoting your way of farming, adding customers who appreciate what you are doing, and, yes, increasing sales of what you produce, you will need to become an expert on the Farm Bill, or at least the parts of it that directly affect your work. Whenever this bill comes up for renewal, which happens about every five years, it attracts major lobbying efforts from every conceivable business affected for better or worse by this legislation. You, or the groups that represent your interests, must be part of that process. The federal dollars now devoted to research and promotion of organic agriculture and other benefits to alternative agriculture, small as they may be, are there only because your fellow farmers did everything possible to advocate for them.

If you are farming sustainably, you are, by definition, an agricultural activist, working with your hands and sweat for a healthier and more sustainable food system. You may not feel like an activist, but because that is how you will be perceived, you might as well start acting like one. Make it part of your daily business and your long-term business plan to advocate for the kind of food system you want to create.

If you don't do this, who will?

I wish you all the courage in the world to take on this challenge.

Marion Nestle is the Paulette Goddard Professor of Nutrition, Food Studies, and Public Health at New York University. She teaches and lectures widely about food policy and advocacy and is the author of several prize-winning books on the politics of food and nutrition, most recently *Soda Politics: Taking on Big Soda (and Winning)*.

RICHARD WISWALL

I'm not sure at what age I realized I wanted to be a farmer, but perhaps it was at some point in my childhood. As kids, my older brother and I were attracted to anything related to homesteading and independent living skills. We pored over every issue of *Mother Earth News*. Makeshift kilns, forges, snare traps, and forts were part of the scenery around home in rural Long Island, New York. Trial-and-error projects, like homemade wine that exploded in our bedroom and leaked down and stained the dining room wall, were memorable, to say the least.

I went to college in Vermont, drawn in part to the state's environmental and back-to-the-land culture. I spent a semester of my junior year in Nepal, living with a subsistence farm family in the Kathmandu Valley and biking an hour to language and culture classes in the city. Trekking in the Himalayas and writing a term paper on the effects of the Green Revolution capped what was a pivotal point in my life.

I returned to college and read Wendell Berry's *The Unsettling of America,* another very big influence on my development as a farmer. Other books, such as *Diet for a Small Planet, Radical Agriculture, Living the Good Life,* and *Limits to Growth*, continued to shape my thoughts. Helen and Scott Nearing came to the college and spoke, and shortly after, my adviser asked me to help on his farm. He put me on a Farmall C to disc a field. That was it: I was hooked.

After graduating, I had the fortunate opportunity to buy into Cate Farm in East Montpelier, Vermont. Four friends and I got together and purchased the farm from a then financially distressed Goddard College. I was only a 5 percent owner, but it allowed me to start my own farm business without a huge mortgage hanging over my head.

I was full of ideas and long on energy and enthusiasm, but short on experience and knowledge. I had grown a garden before, but only on a tiny plot. With lots of help from good friends, I took a shotgun approach to the first year: do a little of lots of different things and see if any hit a target. Trialing eight varieties of green cabbage was a tad excessive, especially considering we were also growing forty other types of vegetables, plus chickens, rabbits, pigs, bees, turkeys, geese, and ducks. What was I thinking? That was thirty-five years ago; hindsight is a wonderful thing.

Although the days were long and the learning curve was steep, I distinctly remember feeling that with farming, anything was possible. If a niche market opened up for asparagus, I'd plant an acre. Or when the Chernobyl nuclear disaster quadrupled the price of Italian radicchio in 1986, I'd be a radicchio farmer. (Both happened.) This reasoning fueled many a farming venture; some succeeded, many did not.

At some point, my idealism collided with economic reality. I was working very long hours for not much financial return. With my appetite to take on new ventures, I found it impossible to juggle all the things that needed to get done. Management by triage propelled the farm forward clumsily, but not in a satisfying way. Money and time were always in short supply. In an urge to succeed, I put in longer and longer days. Something had to change.

In a perfect world, people should be able to farm, make enough to adequately support themselves, and have time off for family and leisure. That doesn't sound too unreasonable. Farming *is* a great way of life, and farmers enjoy their work for lots of good reasons, like working outdoors, being independent, sowing seeds and marveling at the plants that grow, caring for animals, and working with the rhythms of nature. Fundamental satisfaction comes from working the land and producing nutritious, wholesome food for the community. What could be better? Not much, in my opinion.

But when the financial numbers don't line up, farmers, including me, can be famously guilty of self-exploitation. Like many entrepreneurs, farmers believe in what they do so much that they will do what it takes to succeed: work longer and longer hours, sacrifice family and leisure time, balance the books at night so as not to waste precious daylight hours. Deep meaning derived from their work is one of the fuels that keep farmers going despite increasing hardships. But there is a limit to this.

One thing for certain that we all have in common is that we only have twenty-four hours in a day. Some of those hours are for sleeping, eating, family interaction, and domestic chores, and some are for work. *Hours for work are a finite resource.* Our number of work hours reaches a maximum limit at some point.

I tracked daily work hours one spring when my wife and I were short-handed, and we each logged eighty-hour weeks. This represents actual farm work time, not meals or breaks. Although my wife and I were able to do this for a while, it was not sustainable. Meals were simple and quick or skipped; laundry and housecleaning went undone for long stretches; leisure time didn't exist; family and friends were put on hold.

Only because these eighty-hour weeks lasted for a finite period that spring could we do it. That, and knowing we'd be able to make up for lost personal time later in the season.

Here's some sage advice: "Do as I say, not as I did." My point is that it is easy to pile on work hours until it is too late. Work weeks of sixty, seventy, or eighty hours lead to burnout and possibly to giving up farming altogether—not the intended result when you start farming. Finding the right balance between work and nonwork is imperative. In hindsight, my wife and I would have been much better off hiring two helpers. And the same goes for any seventy- or eighty-hour workweek: hire someone to help.

Farmers often believe, "I don't have the money or cash flow to pay an employee." Think about that for a moment. If your farm is not making enough money to pay an employee's wage, how are you going to pay yourself? If the money shortage is only a temporary cash shortfall caused by the seasonal nature of your expense-forward and sales-after business, then borrow some short-term capital to bridge the gap. If it is not just a cash-flow issue, then there's a larger problem. If your farm business doesn't generate enough extra money after you subtract expenses from sales, then how will you add in another expense of paying an employee?

A farm that is profitable over the year generates excess funds after expenses are subtracted from sales. You will need this excess for your basic living expenses of shelter, clothing, and food; hopefully more excess will be left over for things like savings and some fun. Any surplus can also be reinvested in your farm, especially if and when you increase in scale and infrastructure.

Sometimes farmers look at their bottom line at year's end and say, "It isn't great, but I didn't have to commute to work, pay for kids' day care, or buy fancy clothes for work." While that may be true, it's a rationalization for feeling inadequately compensated for a year of hard work and risk.

Farmers can more easily calculate their work effort with a more commonly understood barometer: the hourly wage. We all have a rough sense of what we should be making per hour; for instance, if you weren't farming, $15 or $20 per hour would be what you could earn as a carpenter, landscaper, or restaurant waitstaff.

Take a minute and think about what hourly wage you feel you deserve or is available to you. Don't fall into the trap of the poor-farmer paradigm that says farmers *can't* make money. What wage do you think you'd like to make?

Now look at your yearly tally—sales minus expenses—and divide that number by the hours you worked on the farm. For a normal nine-to-five job, there are forty work hours per week and about fifty weeks per year, for a total of two thousand work-hours a year for regular full-time work. At $10 an hour, that is $20,000 a year; $15 an hour works out to $30,000 a year.

But farmers' hours are not that evenly spaced: from April through October, sixty-hour workweeks are common. In November and December, the work-load decreases to thirty hours a week. And in January, February, and March, at least in the cold climates, the workload may be only twenty hours a week.

That all totals to 2,360 hours for a farmer's work hours a year—a little bit higher than the two thousand hours of a nine-to-five job.

So if you netted $23,600 a year on your farm, you made $10 an hour on average. Good? Bad? You decide. There is no set answer. The hourly wage reference point is one most people easily relate to.

If your response is, "I don't need a lot of money; I'm doing what I love, and that is just the nature of farming," my comeback would be, "If you want to work for next to nothing, come work for me!" *We all need to value ourselves and our time.* Our work hours are limited; use them wisely.

Labor is often a big line item in a farm's budget. This is not necessarily bad; farming is a labor-intensive business. And even if labor is the single biggest expense on your farm, you don't need to trim it as long as labor is being used efficiently and effectively. Where else would you rather spend money? On folks living in your community and supporting local businesses or on some faraway corporation? Don't make the mistake of thinking the large expense of labor means you need to pay substandard wages or work short-handed; just make sure your farm enterprises are profitable enough to pay for that labor.

Building a farm business from scratch is a ton of work. No amount of sugarcoating can hide that fact. The learning curve is steep, and to lift off and attain cruising altitude takes persistence, hard work, and some thinking.

For many years, I acted first, then thought about it second. Couple this with my desire to take on everything at once, and you have one frenetic farmer. Looking back, and also knowing other farmers just starting out, I have a few pieces of advice.

1. Good business practices are essential to a farm's success. Ultimately, we need to be environmentally, socially, and financially sustainable. You can be the best grower, marketer, and innovator, but all that goes out the window if your farm fails financially. Farmers tend to have an allergic reaction to business; they take a head-in-the-sand approach to finances. Take time to work *on* your business, not just *in* your business. Strong farm financials and planning safeguard your stability in the face of unforeseen challenges, such as deflated market prices or extreme weather events.

2. Think first, act second. Business plan or not, take some time to jot down your plans and goals: What do you want to grow or raise? Who will buy it? How will you market it? What will be the gross sales and expenses for the entire farm? How much money is needed for start-up? How long is the payback period for some of these start-up expenditures? Then try to figure out how to put smart money into your bank account by analyzing the costs and benefits of your top sellers. Pencil out any farm enterprise ideas on the back of an envelope. Keep it simple at first: rough in the big numbers of sales and expenses for each farm enterprise you are contemplating. For example, will the sale price of your livestock be enough to cover the costs of young stock, feed, equipment, and labor? Will you be able to pay yourself (or an employee) a living wage and still have some left over for a rainy day?

3. Don't bite off too much at first. Maybe farmers have a genetic defect that drives them to take on too many projects to accomplish them all well. Again, think through the big picture of the entire farm—there is always next year and the year after that to broaden your scope.

4. Learn about business. Your farm is a business, whether you recognize it as one or not. Tackle financial literacy. Delve into balance sheets, profit-and-loss statements, and cash-flow projections. Educate yourself through classes and workshops from farm and business organizations or via the Internet; marketing and management are taught in many places. While the business end of farming is rarely the motivating force to farm, it is as important as any other aspect of farming and critical to success.

5. Think cooperatively. Get to know other farmers around you and strive for a win-win relationship with them. Try not to step on other local farmers' toes; life is too short to be at odds with our neighbors, peers, and colleagues. We all can help one another through knowledge sharing, group purchasing, and marketing.

6. Take a look at your inner motivations. Why are you passionate about farming? To work the land? To be your own boss? To be self-sufficient? To grow great food for yourself and your community? The more deeply defined your desires are, the more likely you will attain them. Conversely, it is hard to get what you want if you don't know what it is. Goal-setting exercises are a good place to start.

Hard work has inherent rewards: a sense of accomplishment, the satisfaction of being productive and working toward an overarching goal. I enjoy a day of hard work just like many other people. And work is necessary for most of us to get by in this world. But work on a farm can be never-ending; the to-do list tends to keep growing. To be successful, we strive to do it all.

Wanting success for your farm is completely natural, and working at something you love makes it feel less like work. But be aware that working too hard can put your life out of whack or burn you out. Keeping the big picture in focus—like writing my own personal mission statement—helps me stay centered: I'm making a living by growing healthy, nutritious food for the community, using sustainable and environmental practices that work with nature and foster the health of the world around us.

Paying attention to all parts of your farm life, including the business side, can reap rewards. A well-run farm business yields a healthy bottom line that pays the farmers and employees well and generates money to reinvest in the farm and to save for a rainy day. A financially stable farm is a resilient farm.

I sincerely hope your farm meets all your expectations, in all regards. Happy farming!

Richard Wiswall has been farming Cate Farm in East Montpelier, Vermont, since 1981, growing certified-organic vegetables, herbs, and flowers. He enjoys helping others with the business side of their farms and is the author of *The Organic Farmer's Business Handbook.*

NICOLAS JAMMET

Dear young farmer,

We're a team. Together we are building a new food system. Such a change requires a new way of thinking—a new infrastructure to make our people and our land healthier. To impact our food system takes courage. To reshape its very foundation takes even more courage. You must believe in your voice and move us toward a future that most people don't see.

If you feel like you are on this path alone, rest assured, you are not. This new generation of the food system is composed of diners, chefs, producers, entrepreneurs, and thought leaders, but at the core is you—the farmer. You're the one planting the seeds of change.

Know that you have a voice and that it's the most important one in the game. You listen to the land, and you speak for the land. But you need allies. You need to team up with partners in the food space so we can build businesses to support the movement. We can redefine what people eat and what people want. We can change the food system together.

Although the industrialization and commoditization of food have had unfortunate consequences for our health and the environment, we're in the midst of a paradigm shift. We are fortunate to be in this position as the world of food is changing—and to be driving that change. Consumers have started to learn about their food and are demanding that it be better and its production more transparent. The link between our food and our health is becoming more apparent. The link between our farms and our tables needs to do the same. This link starts in your soil. As the next generation of farmers, you hold the health of our nation in your hands and in your fields.

To build a truly sustainable food system, the fates of the entrepreneur and the farmer must be interdependent. We started sweetgreen nine years ago with a desire to change the way people think about food and to positively affect the food system. We believe the choices we make every day about what we eat, where it comes from, and how it's made have powerful consequences for the health of individuals, communities, and the planet. That food ethos calls for an approach to food and sourcing that's fallen by the wayside in the modern food economy. We are part of the *new* food economy, and our business only grows as our network of farmers grows—and as *their* businesses grow.

You, the next generation of farmers, should know that you have partners in this new era. For every young farmer in this country, there exists a young food entrepreneur, chef, or consumer who is aligned with your values. When we can make these connections, we strengthen our food system and invest in our soil, preserving the system for years to come.

My advice to you is to find your partners in this new movement and forge relationships with buyers, chefs, and entrepreneurs. Find partners who will work with you day in and day out, who will stick with you through storms and downturns. Together, you will have the ability to rethink what you're growing—and why. Don't build your business around consumer demands; grow what will make the farm, soil, and consumer healthier, given the region and climate you're in. Let the land dictate the trend. If you do this in partnership with like-minded individuals and businesses, you'll create demand for new foods and introduce more sustainable choices to the consumer palate.

These partners exist today, and their ranks will only grow in the coming years. Connecting with them brings incredible value to both sides and paves a path toward a better food system. Each connection we make fortifies the foundation for a new way of growing, eating, and thinking about food—and it can't be done alone.

Let's do it together.

Nicolas Jammet is cofounder and co-CEO of sweetgreen, a destination for simple, seasonal, and healthy food. Jammet has been recognized as a key innovator in food and business, named to *Inc.*'s "30 Under 30," *Forbes*'s "30 Under 30," and *Food & Wine*'s "40 Big Food Thinkers 40 and Under." In 2015 First Lady Michelle Obama selected Jammet for the Presidential Delegation to Expo 2015, an international summit to discuss global nutrition and health and sustainable food solutions.

MAS MASUMOTO

—

Dear Nikiko,

When I came back to the farm after college, I was lost, confused, and heartbroken. I know, this sounds like a bad country-western song, yet as with a good ballad, there's a story here. Now that you, my daughter, are coming home to the farm after graduate school, I hope you're ready for a journey into the world of farming, business, nature, and perhaps most important, a quest to forge your identity and find yourself.

You'll begin with a search.

My father, your grandfather, was not a storyteller. While I worked side by side with him in the fields, he remained quiet and reserved, embodying the typical image of the stoic old farmer. It drove me crazy—like the time he told me about the boxes of dynamite in our barn.

"What dynamite?" I asked. It wasn't the typical farm tool I had seen in books about growing up on a farm.

He nodded, and we had to finish the row before another sentence. Or was this a way he tricked me into working faster?

My father expressed himself with his shovel, through long hours methodically moving up and down each row, tending to every tree and vine. His actions spoke the loudest—quiet acts whose meaning took years to grasp. Silence was the hardest language to comprehend. Yet understanding that code proved to be the secret to our farming. To work the land quietly. To labor in solitude. Muted, paced, tenacious, restrained. A type of tranquility: working with nature. And naturally, alone. (Sometimes too alone? Most farmers like to be by themselves, and I find myself slipping into unsociable behavior. And liking it.)

That's when I truly became the student. I remember learning how to prune. Your grandfather quickly demonstrated by first walking around part of the tree, positioning the ladder and beginning to clip, chop, snip, slice. Wood fell, and a balanced and strong structure of branches seemed to magically appear. He repeated the process, whacking some, trimming others, and again, a shaped tree was carved out from the mass of tangled limbs. He explained little, modeled his work, repeated, and moved on. I longed for the college lecture.

I had to first learn how to see. I made notes—some mental and others on a notepad—tucking away each lesson. Yet only when I myself tried to prune did my education begin. When you farm, you have to learn how to see the future.

I returned to that same tree every year, and I could learn from one more year of growth and harvest. Sadly, the best lessons were when I pruned a limb poorly, resulting in too few peaches or weak ones that did not size well. Worst of all, my mistakes were public; I felt everyone could see them. Once, one of the workers heckled me when he questioned, "Who pruned that tree?" The crew laughed. I was no longer the *patrón* and not even a very good farmhand. At least it boosted the workers' egos, as it should.

Repetition is the natural rhythm of farming. The lessons continue today, even in my sixties. And the learning may never stop. I try to convince myself it's the secret to feeling young. To have the privilege of study implies there's a future when lessons can be put to use.

Your grandfather left his fingerprints all over this land. The mounds of hardpan rock piled along a ditch bank. The welded seams on old equipment that hold fast after decades. A cement irrigation valve, patched and repatched after an impatient teenage son broke it with a speeding tractor. Work defined my father, me, and our fields. Work will define you as a farmer.

I once heard a slogan on a radio ad from an era when the daily morning farm report was broadcast and accompanied our breakfast. The ad announced: "Your grandfather farmed with his back. Your father with machines. You'll have to learn to farm with your head."

Today, I'm not sure much has changed except that you, my daughter, will have to do all three. You cannot escape the hard, physical work. No peach or nectarine or grape simply grows by itself. Contrary to the promise of new technologies, farming will require hand labor.

You'll also benefit from equipment that makes life easier. The industrial revolution still unfolds on farms with new inventions—and all the while you'll be required to work faster, cover more ground, produce more efficiently. Like in Alice in Wonderland, you'll run to stay in place, and to go anywhere, you'll simply have to run twice as fast. Your challenge may be how to make old equipment work with modern demands.

The age of technology has forever altered our landscape. Computers can dig up information and knowledge that was out of reach before. You can communicate with others—fellow farmers, researchers, buyers, consumers—like I never could. You'll now know more, and will need to know more.

What will the farm movie from the future look like? Will the desolate landscapes of climate change create a world where dirt farmers barely scratch out a living, in contrast to the class division of urban techies and their extreme wealth and entitlement—*Hunger Games 2.0*? What will the future *Field of Dreams* look like? Dreadlocked coders and skateboarders stepping out of pools of slime on a megafarm dairy operation?

Remember, sometimes ignorance allows you to accept your mistakes and live with errors. And technology is only a tool; people are still required. People grow food. People make food.

If all goes well, one day in the future, look up from shoveling weeds or adjusting a disc blade or studying a weather pattern on a smartphone (or embedded on your contact lens or the newest techie device). Pause to witness the decades of work that have passed and how sustainable farming builds life: the soil will be healthier, the orchards and vineyard stronger than ever, and you will have carved out a niche from the earth. Your blind faith will have accomplished much. Take the moment to celebrate: small-scale farming can coexist with Big Ag! The public will support farms with great stories of authenticity and meaning! Then you'll look down, return to the task at hand, and realize more work still needs to be done. Depressing. Exhausting. Relentless. And yet somehow renewing; otherwise you would have quit long ago or found a partner who was naive enough to support this Kafkaesque dream we live.

Finally, I believe that it's only when you grow older that a change transpires. Maybe it's because you physically slow down, or your perception of success changes, or you accept your position in life. You may be more content with what you have instead of what you don't possess.

Images of new equipment fade as you develop a relationship with your old tools. You'll appreciate the character of our old tractor and the secret technique to start that ancient Ford. You'll be comfortable repairing the disc ridger brackets and finally will have learned to stockpile a can full of category three bolts that don't break as easily. You'll be willing to accept less productivity and start measuring new ways of a return on investment beyond the metric of money. All the lessons that I inherited from your grandfather, you'll have absorbed via a magical farmer-to-farmer osmosis—by working with your old man.

When younger, I would have never believed that a type of maturity comes with age; that wisdom comes with experience, hard lessons from hard work; that mistakes contribute to a wealth of knowledge. To ignore things that are out of your control and go forward with blind optimism—that will often lead to failure. (Remember that old, morbid joke circulating in our fields: "They did a series of autopsies on old farmers and when they opened them up, they were full of 'next years.'") And on this piece of land, a native competency will grow. My father, your grandfather, came to know this well.

One day you'll talk to your trees and vines, and they may even, in their own way, talk back as you read the color of their leaves, the vigor of their roots, the scent of a ripening fruit. And you'll accept the option of euthanasia for those ready to be put out of production—a new alternative I find myself considering more and more as I age. You'll learn that it's okay to miss them, and that's the secret to letting go.

I'm a fool to think another birthday automatically makes you better—a belief some adopt that age gives you license. It may do the opposite, causing people to become narrower in their thinking. Instead, it's about an acceptance of who you are and the value of reflection. A celebration of thought and life. Allow yourself contemplation. Meditation. Reconciliation. Of the self.

Something does change with each passing year, especially now that I have turned sixty. I can't yet fully explain but a moment of clarity accompanied my own health scare. (Triple bypass heart surgery can make one rethink life.) Now a question weighs on me yet excites me every morning: how many harvests do I have left?

What you leave behind matters, and it's not about money, wealth, or material goods. It's not success you want to be remembered for, but significance.

Does that revelation change how I farm? Wonderfully, not much, because I think I had all along tried to do what I felt was right, worked with passion, and respected the world. We lost money, but we did it naturally and organically; somehow that made it different. (Of course, that couldn't go on for too long. I may be naive, but not dumb.)

We had many moments of frustration and disappointment. Self-doubt had to be harvested every year, and it took a toll at times. But I'm not as angry as I used to be. I sense you'll experience something similar as you tackle new challenges like climate change. Accept, adapt, and advance: a simple strategy of transformation that does not always fit today's world of politics and policy. But you may witness an entirely different world of growing and composting that you'll need to master.

We believed in keeping old, heirloom peach and nectarine varieties the world had forsaken. We too became forsaken, but with luck and sweat, we found homes for the homeless. We built the farm from the earth up, adding life to the dirt and hardpan fields while renewing the soul of the land. We experimented, allowed for failures, and kept learning from our mistakes. We grew to understand the power of story to motivate, guide, and even brand ourselves.

I leave behind stories. A tale you're now part of, a narrative you'll write with your own words. If we're fortunate, the cycle ends with a story of trust in the community of people surrounding our operation and family—a belief in who we are and what we do.

Then, a final amazing epiphany: the cycle repeats itself. An ironic discovery. Like growing things, the new crop simply begins again. Over and over. Every season. Every harvest. Every generation.

Love,
Your father

Mas Masumoto, along with his daughter, Nikiko, farms eighty acres of organic peaches, nectarines, and raisins outside of Fresno, California. He is the author of nine books, including *Epitaph for a Peach* and *Wisdom of the Last Farmer*. Their family farm is the subject of a PBS documentary film, *Changing Season*.

ACKNOWLEDGMENTS

So many people helped bring this book to life.

Deepest thanks to the authors for the gift of their time, words, and passion for the subject of farming and all that it touches in the world. The views and opinions they express are theirs alone, and for them, we are most grateful.

Warmest thanks to friends in the Stone Barns Center community who helped catalyze the book and its contributors, especially Rob Shaeffer for his patience and encouragement, as well as Aleah Papes, Fred Kirschenmann, and Sam Anderson. For their counsel and outreach, thanks also to Rick and Beth Schnieders, Irene Hamburger, Alicia Harvey, and Carolyn Mugar. Many thanks to the Stone Barns Center team for their enthusiasm for the project, and to the Board of Directors, under the leadership of Peggy Dulany, for their good faith and support.

And with gratitude to the true North Star of this project: all the farmers, young and not so young, both practicing and aspiring, with whom we've had the pleasure of working and becoming friends. This project is rooted in all that you grow and hope to realize in this life.

Jill Isenbarger and **Martha Hodgkins**
Stone Barns Center for Food and Agriculture

CODA

Manifesto: The Mad Farmer Liberation Front
by Wendell Berry

Love the quick profit, the annual raise,
vacation with pay. Want more
of everything ready-made. Be afraid
to know your neighbors and to die.
And you will have a window in your head.
Not even your future will be a mystery
any more. Your mind will be punched in a card
and shut away in a little drawer.
When they want you to buy something
they will call you. When they want you
to die for profit they will let you know.
So, friends, every day do something
that won't compute. Love the Lord.
Love the world. Work for nothing.
Take all that you have and be poor.
Love someone who does not deserve it.
Denounce the government and embrace
the flag. Hope to live in that free
republic for which it stands.
Give your approval to all you cannot
understand. Praise ignorance, for what man
has not encountered he has not destroyed.
Ask the questions that have no answers.
Invest in the millennium. Plant sequoias.
Say that your main crop is the forest
that you did not plant,
that you will not live to harvest.

Say that the leaves are harvested
when they have rotted into the mold.
Call that profit. Prophesy such returns.
Put your faith in the two inches of humus
that will build under the trees
every thousand years.
Listen to carrion—put your ear
close, and hear the faint chattering
of the songs that are to come.
Expect the end of the world. Laugh.
Laughter is immeasurable. Be joyful
though you have considered all the facts.
So long as women do not go cheap
for power, please women more than men.
Ask yourself: Will this satisfy
a woman satisfied to bear a child?
Will this disturb the sleep
of a woman near to giving birth?
Go with your love to the fields.
Lie easy in the shade. Rest your head
in her lap. Swear allegiance
to what is nighest your thoughts.
As soon as the generals and the politicos
can predict the motions of your mind,
lose it. Leave it as a sign
to mark the false trail, the way
you didn't go. Be like the fox
who makes more tracks than necessary,
some in the wrong direction.
Practice resurrection.

"Manifesto: The Mad Farmer Liberation Front" from *The Country of Marriage*, Harcourt Brace Jovanovich, Inc., 1973. Also published by Counterpoint Press in *The Selected Poems of Wendell Berry*, 1999; *The Mad Farmer Poems*, 2008; *New Collected Poems*, 2012.

GLOSSARY

CSA (community-supported agriculture): A farm-share program through which small farmers sell their products directly to individuals, who receive a share of the farm's bounty, usually weekly, throughout the growing season. CSAs have also sprung up offering seafood, meat, bread, and other items.

certified organic: Production methods certified as organic by the US Department of Agriculture, following a defined set of standards describing how farmers grow crops and raise livestock and which materials they may use. These standards cover the product from farm to table, including soil and water quality, pest control processes, livestock practices, and rules for food additives.

foodways: The study of what, how, and why we eat, encompassing issues of race, class, gender, economy, environment, geography, and history, among others.

GMO (genetically modified organism): A plant, animal, or microorganism whose genetic material (DNA) has been altered in a way that does not occur through mating and/ or natural recombination. This process allows selected individual genes to be transferred from one organism into another, sometimes between nonrelated species. Foods produced from or using genetically modified organisms are often referred to as GM foods.

greenwash: Disinformation disseminated by an organization or a corporation so as to present an environmentally responsible public image.

organic agriculture: A system of production based on methods that preserve the environment and avoid most synthetic materials such as pesticides and antibiotics.

USAID: US Agency for International Development.

USDA: US Department of Agriculture.

WWOOFer: A volunteer in World Wide Opportunities on Organic Farms, a movement linking volunteers with organic farmers and growers to promote cultural and educational experiences based on trust and nonmonetary exchanges, thereby helping to build a sustainable global community.